P9-DFS-243

A WOK A WEEK
52 LITE & EASY MEALS

For Paul,

Thank you for working with me — Enjoy!

Elizabeth

A WOK
A WEEK

52 LITE & EASY MEALS

ELIZABETH CHIU KING & DONNA H. DEAN

Copyright © 1998 by Elizabeth Chiu King

Photograph © 1998 by Janine Menlove

All rights reserved. No part of this book may be reproduced or transmitted in any form or by any means, electronic or mechanical, including photocopying, recording or by any information storage and retrieval system, except brief excerpts for the purpose of review, without written permission of the publisher.

China Books & Periodicals, Inc.
2929 Twenty-Fourth Street
San Francisco, CA 94110
USA

Cover design by Mary E. Bush
Cover photo by Janine Menlove
Interior design by Donna H. Dean
Brush drawings by Xi'an Lin
Pen and ink illustrations by Iris Shen-Van Buren
Nutrient analysis by Bob Wilson

First Edition, March 1998, San Francisco
Library of Congress Catalog Card Number: 97-77607
ISBN 0-8351-2630-7
Printed in Malaysia

Dedication

Elizabeth:

To my mother, Rowena, and to my amah, Ah Woo,
for nurturing me with love and food and
for teaching me how to cook.

Donna:

To my husband, Dale Haller,
who gently encourages, sustains, and challenges me.
And to my mother, Louise, who taught me to laugh and to not give up.

Acknowledgments

So many friends have given enormous help to Donna and me as we worked on this book over the years. In particular, I must thank Joy Taylor-Skiba, David McCarthy, Bob and Faye Levine, Paula Zemel, Robin Mather, Brian Carroll, Corinne Abatt, Doris Chang, Shirley Lau, Nona Dreyer, Diana M. Chang, Philomena Hsieh, Ginka Gerova-Ortega, Jan Jaffrey, Jules Toner, S.J., Jack Schuett, S.J., Chandriga Raman and Bonnie Stone.

Special thanks go out to Theresa Shen who introduced me to my publisher and the very helpful Greg Jones.

As always, I am grateful to my friend and coauthor, Donna Dean, who stuck with me through "thick and thin" – writing, editing, designing, testing, and revising version after version – until we were able to complete a book we can both present with pride.

Others offered important contributions to the "look of the book": Janine Menlove contributed her excellent photographs, X'ian Lin enlivens the book with her brush drawings, and Iris Shen-Van Buren adds delight and clarity with her pen and ink illustrations.

Bob Wilson deserves special thanks for his meticulous work on the nutritional analyses.

My assistant, Dawn Li, also deserves special mention for her tireless proofing and organizing efforts.

Last, but not least, my love and gratitude embrace my husband Albert, our children Albert, Jr., and his wife, Siew-ling, Tom, and his fiancée, Marlowe Muske, and our wonderful grandson, Ian.
Their love and support – along with all these other fine people – have made this book possible.

Contents

Listing of Recipes

Listing of Recipes

The Magic Cooking Utensil

The wok is, indeed, a magic cooking utensil! It is suitable for stir-tossing, stir-frying, boiling, deep-frying and almost any other cooking method you might choose. The wok comes in many shapes and sizes and can be made of a number of different materials. The carbon steel wok is the least expensive and most practical – but it must be well-seasoned before use. Catalphon– heavy-gauged aluminum that is electrochemically treated – is more expensive, but you may find it worth the added expense because it heats so well.

To Season a New Carbon Steel Wok

Scrub the wok thoroughly with kitchen cleanser and hot water to remove the protective coat of oil, Dry it thoroughly over low heat and add two tablespoons of cooking coil. Fold several sheets of paper towels into a small square and rub the oil all over the inside of the seal to seal the pores. Heat the wok thoroughly for another 15 minutes, rotating it from side to side so that the entire wok is coated with oil as it heats. Wipe it dry with paper towels. Repeat the process of coating, heating, and wiping until the paper towels are not longer discolored after wiping the wok. *Your wok is now ready for use!*

To Clean a Seasoned Wok

Simply wash the wok in hot water, using a mild dish soap if necessary and – if necessary, brush scrub it with a hard-bristle brush. *Never use a scouring pad.* Dry the wok over low heat before putting it away. This prevents rusting. If your wok should become rusty, scrub off the rust with a cleansing powder and repeat the seasoning process. *Do not put a seasoned wok in the dishwasher.*

Accessories for the Wok Include

A domelike lid, and a long-handled metal spoon or metal spatula. If your stove is electric, a flat-bottomed wok fits better. A 14-inch wok works best for most dishes.

If It's Tuesday, It Must Be Chinese!

Take these ingredients and add them all together. Stir well, taste test over and over, add quite a few laughs and quite a few tears and you will come up with *A WOK A WEEK:*

- *A woman born in Shanghai, China*
- *A woman born in Urbana, Illinois*
- *A gourmet Chinese cook who can prepare anything*
- *An average American cook who likes delicious yet simple recipes*
- *An author who has already published two successful cookbooks*
- *A health educator who demands that cookbooks be low in fat*
- *A wife who prepares Chinese food everyday*
- *A wife who feels her weekly American meal plan needs "a lift"*
- *Two very busy friends who need to cook in a hurry*
- *Two fussy eaters who want the tastiest, healthiest and easiest-to-prepare meals.*

We have struggled for six years to bring this book to fruition. We have cooked and written and analyzed and recooked and rewritten and reanalyzed until we wondered why we ever started. Probably we would have given it all up except for the fact that we are both too stubborn and we had the cheery support of our meticulous nutrient analyst, Bob Wilson.

Getting a cookbook published these days is not a lark. Bookstores abound with cook-books. Publishers cast a jaded eye on any new effort. *Yet we knew we had something unique. No one had published a cookbook with classic Chinese recipes that were low-fat and adapted to the American need for "quick and easy."* How could we woo a publisher to help us bring you this book?

One afternoon when we were sitting in a Portland marketplace, a bit dejected and calling on the Spirit to inspire us with a fresh approach, we hit upon a novel organizing concept. Why not present our recipes as menus? Why not organize them on a one-meal-a-week calendar so that instead of "meat loaf on Tuesday" it could be something totally new – a Chinese meal? Why not call our new book A WOK A WEEK?

We both loved this approach. Organizing the recipes into meals helps the newcomer to Chinese cooking know how to combine dishes. It also helps the cook learn to plan combinations of dishes that keep the meal's total calories from fat down to 30% or less. Our menu approach serves as a guide. Still, you are free to create your own menus.

Our monthly calendar of meals highlights balance and seasonal variety as the user moves through the year. *No meal is repeated in the 52 recipes of* A WOK A WEEK. Yet *recipes* are repeated in new meal combinations so that the average cook can learn more about our Chinese style of balancing color, texture, shapes, flavors and presentations.

We have taken the difficulty out of Chinese cooking. The Chinese ingredients I use are easy to find in your local supermarket. Cutting and chopping are minimized. Cooking techniques are limited to those familiar to the average American cook.

You will need no fancy equipment, although we do recommend you invest in a wok and steamer, if you don't already have them. And once you become a true wok-a-week cook, you'll probably want the added convenience of a rice cooker.

When we of the Chinese culture greet each other, we almost immediately ask, "Have you eaten?" Good food shared with good humor is central to our culture. We hope this small book will bring much happiness and good health to your home.

Elizabeth 邱文慈

Chopping

In *A WOK A WEEK* chopping is reduced to a minimum. As you learn a few basics you will master an ancient art designed for beauty of presentation and quick cooking.

The basics:

- **KNIFE/CLEAVER:** Keep your knife or cleaver razor-sharp.

- **FINE-CUTTING MEATS, SEAFOOD & POULTRY:** Partially freezing meat, seafood and poultry before fine-cutting makes them easier to cut.

- **STRAIGHT/DIAGONAL CHOPPING:** Keep your knife or cleaver at right angles to the food. Diagonal slicing gives vegetables a greater cooking surface and adds to the beauty. Make your slices thin, about ¼ to ⅛ of an inch.

- **JULIENNE/MATCH STICKS:** First cut the food into ⅛-inch thick slices. Stack the slices and then cut them into ⅛-inch long match sticks.

- **DICED/CUBES:** First cut the food into ½ or 1-inch-thick slices. Stack the slices and then cut them into square cubes. In this cookbook cubes are assumed to be 1-inch square; diced food is ½-inch square.

Cooking Methods

Most techniques used in *A WOK A WEEK* are familiar to you: baking, blending/mixing, boiling, broiling, braising, cold-tossing (like tossing a salad), grilling, microwaving, poaching, and roasting. The only two techniques that need a little explanation are steaming and stir-tossing.

- **STEAMING:** A healthy way to prepare delicious food. Those of you who know this technique have experienced its benefits: it retains the nutrient value, texture and good flavor of the food while it heightens the color. Steam slowly cooks and tenderizes marinated meat, fowl and seafood.

  When you find you enjoy steamed food, invest in a Chinese steamer – either an aluminum or bamboo one. The aluminum steamer comes with a pot for the water, two perforated racks and a lid. The bamboo steamer comes with one or two racks and a lid. The racks fit nicely over most standard dutch oven pots or in your wok.

- **STIR-TOSSING:** A modified low-fat version of stir-frying. Cut the food as directed in the recipe. Follow the directions for marinating. Heat your wok to about 400 degrees, add only 1 tablespoon of oil, swirl to coat the wok. Quickly add and stir-toss the food, following the sequence and timing in the recipe. Then add the sauce, broth or binder to give the dish additional moisture and flavor and to prevent scorching.

Chinese Ingredients

Many Chinese ingredients are now common items on supermarket shelves: soy sauce, canned water chestnuts, wonton wrappers, curry powder, Maggi Seasoning, and sesame seeds. Those listed below are carried in some supermarkets and are always available in Chinese or Oriental markets. *For easy reference they are listed in alphabetical order by the names used in the recipes.*

- **CHINESE DRIED BLACK MUSHROOMS (DRIED SHIITAKE MUSHROOMS):** Before slicing or cooking, soak these dried mushrooms in warm water. Though expensive, they weigh little – so you get a lot for your money – and they add a unique flavor to the dish. *They store indefinitely in a refrigerated, tightly covered container.*

- **CHINESE BROCCOLI (*GAILAN*):** A luscious, crunchy hybrid of broccoli and kale. Great fiber and flavor.

- **FIVE-SPICE POWDER:** A reddish-brown powder made from ground cinnamon, cloves, fennel, dried peppercorn and star anise. *Keeps indefinitely on the shelf.*

- **GLASSY NOODLES (MUNG BEAN THREAD):** Packaged in dry bundles, these noodles must be soak in cold water before cooking. During soaking the noodles become transparent. *The dry noodles keep indefinitely on the shelf.*

- **HOISIN SAUCE:** A thick reddish-brown sweet sauce made from wheat flour, soy beans, sugar, garlic, chili paste, and vinegar. Hoisin sauce is a delicious seasoning and dipping sauce. *Stores for months in a tightly-covered, refrigerated bottle or jar.*

- **HUNAN CHILI PASTE:** A fiery and pungent condiment made from soy beans red hot chili, garlic, and other spices. Hunan Chili Paste is both a seasoning and a dip. *Stores for months in a tightly-covered, refrigerated bottle or jar.*

- **JASMINE RICE:** So named because of its fragrant aroma, this rice cooks just like regular white rice.

- **OYSTER-FLAVORED SAUCE:** A dark-brown, thick sauce made from soy sauce, corn starch, and other seasonings. Oyster-flavored sauce blends and enriches food flavors and imparts a velvety texture to the finished dish. (Donna's friends are especially fond of this sauce.) *Stores indefinitely in the bottle when refrigerated.*

- **PEPPERCORNS (DRIED SICHUAN PEPPERCORNS):** Products of the Sichuan region of China, these reddish-brown peppercorns are highly aromatic and mildly hot. The Chinese usually combine them with whole star anise for a special and favorite seasoning. *They store indefinitely on the shelf in covered containers.*

- **SESAME SEED OIL:** Made from toasted sesame seeds, this oil serves as an ingredient in salad dressings and as a flavoring agent. *It is seldom used as a cooking oil* because it is expensive and smokes at a lower temperature. *Stores indefinitely on the shelf in a tightly covered bottle.*

- **STRAW MUSHROOMS:** Cultivated in beds of straw and usually sold canned, these delightful wee fellows add a delicate flavor to any dish. *Leftover portions keep for about a week when stored in water, covered, and refrigerated.*

52 Lite & Easy Meals –
One a Week Throughout the Year

- Would you like to make Chinese dining a part of your weekly routine? Without the expense of restaurant meals?

- Would you like to expand your Chinese cooking repertoire? Feel as comfortable with your wok and Chinese recipes as you do preparing an Italian or German meal?

- If so, A WOK A WEEK is the book you've been waiting for.

A WOK A WEEK is organized like a calendar – each week we present a new meal of 3 delicious dishes; each month features four meals. No need to flip through a cookbook looking for recipes that are delicious, easy to cook, and go well together – we've done that for you!

Part of the art of Chinese cooking, is:

- Knowing which dishes go together – and

- Learning to carefully balance colors and textures and flavors.

To help you develop these skills, we repeat each recipe at least once in another month's menus. This repetition invites you to practice making the dish again in a new combination of complementary dishes. Following this method you will develop a sense of "what goes with what" and soon be able to create your own menus with comfort and confidence.

However, a skillful cook is only as good as her recipes. Our elegant collection of low-fat gourmet recipes will make you the pride of your family and friends.

- Each recipe has been tested and re-tested to outrageously lower the fat – up to 67% lower in fat than most traditional Chinese dishes! – while maintaining or enhancing the flavor.

- All meals and most recipes are 30% or less fat.

- Each recipe is followed by a nutrient analysis. At a glance you will know if you are keeping your dietary fat to 30% or less as the American Heart Association and the Surgeon General recommend.

- Portions are generous – not "diet-sized" – yet still kind to the heart *and* waistline because the total calories and calories from fat remain low.

- The preparation and cooking process for each recipe has been simplified and timed again and again. Preparation and cooking times are listed to help you plan your meal.

Enjoy adding our Chinese dishes to your weekly meal plan – and invite us over to dinner!

week January

1 Chicken with Anise & Peppercorns
Shanghai String Bean Salad
Fragrant Rice

2 Spicy Steamed Shrimp
Chinese Tossed Salad
White Rice

3 Beef & Onions in Oyster Sauce
Stir-Tossed Potato & Carrot Sticks
Noodles with Bean Sprouts & Scallions

4 Tofu with Crab & Straw Mushrooms
Eggplant in Savory Sauce
Brown Rice

January week 1

Chicken with Anise & Peppercorns
Shanghai String Bean Salad
Fragrant Rice
339 Calories/ 72 Calories from Fat/ 21% Calories from Fat

Chicken with Anise & Peppercorns

A gentle way to cook chicken that will delight your diners. Use this recipe to prepare cooked chicken to use in many other dishes: appetizers, soups, salads and sandwiches.

4 chicken thighs, about 1½ pounds

MARINADE
1 teaspoon sugar
½ teaspoon salt
½ teaspoon black pepper
2 tablespoon dry white wine
1 tablespoon white vinegar
½ tablespoon anise pieces or 4 dried star anise, broken into small pieces
½ tablespoon dry peppercorns

1. Wash the chicken thighs and pat them dry with paper towels. Leave the skin on the thighs to retain the moisture, but trim off the fat and any excess skin. Place the thighs in a shallow dish that fits into your steamer and set aside. Mix the marinade ingredients in a small bowl and spread evenly over the chicken. Let it stand for at least 2 hours. Overnight marinating is even better.

2. Fill a Chinese steamer to the halfway mark with hot tap water. Cover the steamer and bring the water to

a rolling boil in about 10 minutes. Place the dish of chicken on the steamer rack, and put the rack in the steamer. Cover and steam on high for 40 minutes. Do not lift the lid during steaming.

3. Let the chicken cool for 10 minutes before serving.

PREPARATION TIME:	*12-15 minutes*
MARINATING TIME:	*A minimum of 2 hours, overnight marinating is better.*
COOKING TIME:	*50 minutes*
COOLING TIME:	*10 minutes*

EACH SERVING: 176 Calories/ 47 Calories from Fat/ 28% Calories from Fat

Shanghai String Bean Salad

A fail-proof recipe for fresh green beans. For maximum flavor, prepare this dish the day before.

1 pound fresh green beans
2 quarts cold water

DRESSING
½ teaspoon sugar
⅛ teaspoon black pepper
2 tablespoons wine vinegar
2 tablespoons Maggi seasoning
½ tablespoon sesame seed oil
1 teaspoon minced garlic

1. Place the cold water in a large saucepan with a lid and bring to a boil, in about 5 minutes. While the water is boiling, snip off the ends of the beans with a pair of kitchen shears. Wash, drain and set them aside.

2. Mix the dressing ingredients in a large bowl and set aside.

3. When the water is boiling, add the beans, cover and cook on high for 5 minutes. Drain and refresh them in cold water to stop the cooking. Add the beans to the bowl with the dressing. Toss to coat them well. Refrigerate, covered, for an hour or overnight. Tossing the beans from time to time helps the dressing seep into the beans.

PREPARATION TIME:	*6-8 minutes*
COOKING TIME:	*10 minutes*
REFRIGERATION:	*1 hour or overnight*
SERVES:	*4*

EACH SERVING: 64 Calories/ 17 Calories from Fat/ 25% Calories from Fat

Fragrant Rice

Using jasmine rice instead of regular long grain rice introduces a fragrance the Chinese call *Hsiang mi*, "fragrant rice." Our recipe sweetens the pot even more by adding celery, scallions and cilantro and using chicken broth instead of water.

1 cup jasmine rice
1 teaspoon oil
3 stalks of celery, diced (preferably stalks near the heart)
1½ cups chicken broth
2 tablespoons diced scallions
2 tablespoons minced cilantro or Chinese parsley
½ teaspoon freshly ground white pepper

1. Put the rice in a large bowl and rinse it twice in cold water. Pour off the excess water by cupping your hand over the rice grains. Do not use a colander. Set aside.

2. Heat a 2-quart saucepan, add the oil and swirl it for 15 seconds to coat the pan. Add the celery and stir-toss for 45 seconds. Add the chicken broth and bring it to a boil. Add the rice and bring the pot to a second boil. Boil until the broth bubbles to the top, about 3 minutes. Turn the heat to medium and continue cooking, uncovered. Stir occasionally to prevent sticking.

3. When the broth is mostly evaporated (after about 5 minutes) reduce the heat to simmer, cover the pot with a tight-fitting lid and steam for 20 minutes more. Do not lift the lid during this time.

4. When the steaming is complete, fluff the rice, mix in the scallions, cilantro and pepper, fluff again, and serve immediately.

PREPARATION TIME: *5 minutes*
COOKING TIME: *31 minutes*
SERVES: *8 (½ cup servings)*

EACH SERVING: 99 Calories/ 8 Calories from Fat/ 9% Calories from Fat

week 2

Spicy Steamed Shrimp
Chinese Tossed Salad, White Rice
235 Calories/ 9 Calories from Fat/ 4% Calories from Fat

Spicy Steamed Shrimp

Sheer simplicity and elegance! The 5-spice powder (a compound of star anise, peppercorns, fennel, cloves and cinnamon) adds a singular fragrance and dimension to this dish.

1 pound medium shrimp in the shell, raw
4 tablespoons diced scallions

MARINADE
½ tablespoon cornstarch
½ teaspoon 5-spice powder
¼ teaspoon salt
¼ teaspoon sugar
⅛ teaspoon black pepper
2 tablespoons dry white wine

DIPPING SAUCE
¼ cup wine vinegar
¼ cup chicken or fish broth
2 tablespoons lite soy sauce
2 tablespoons diced scallions
½ tablespoon minced garlic
1 teaspoon grated gingerroot

1. Wash and drain, but do not peel the shrimp. Pat them dry with paper towels. Using kitchen shears, make a shallow cut along the spine of each shrimp to make them easier to peel when served. Shrimp this size do not need to be deveined.

2. Mix the marinade ingredients in a large heatproof bowl that fits comfortably on the steamer rack. Add the shrimp to the marinade, mix well, and let stand for 30 minutes or longer.

3. Mix the dipping sauce in a serving bowl and set it aside.

4. Fill a Chinese steamer to the halfway mark with hot water from the tap. Cover the steamer and bring it to a rolling boil in about 10 minutes.

5. When the water in the steamer comes to a rolling boil, (and the shrimp has marinated for at least 30 minutes) place the steamer rack and bowl with the shrimp in the steamer. Cover and steam on high for 8 minutes – or until the shrimp turn pink. Remove them from the steamer and serve steaming hot with the dipping sauce.

PREPARATION TIME: *8-10 minutes*
MARINATING TIME: *30 minutes*

COOKING TIME: 8 minutes
SERVES: 4

EACH SERVING: 98 Calories/ 7 Calories from Fat/ 7% Calories from Fat

Chinese Tossed Salad

Combine your favorite lettuce (iceberg, romaine, bib, Boston) with bok choy and Napa cabbage, add straw mushrooms for elegance and pizazz and enjoy tossed green salad Chinese style.

¾ pound lettuce
¼ pound bok choy
¼ pound Napa cabbage
½ sweet red pepper
1 8-ounce can tiny peeled straw mushrooms, drained

1. Chill individual salad plates.

2. Rinse the greens and break them into bite-sized pieces or cut them on the bias into strips. Toss and mix the greens in a large bowl and then dish them out onto the chilled plates.

3. Trim the pepper and thin slice it into strips. Add several strips to each plate for color and flavor.

4. Top each serving with a tablespoon scoop of straw mushrooms and serve with a side bowl of Quick Sweet and Sour Dressing.

PREPARATION TIME: 6 to 8 minutes
COOKING TIME: None
SERVES: 8
NOTE: *The tiny peeled straw mushrooms are the most attractive. Ask your Chinese grocer for that special variety.*

EACH SERVING: 24 Calories/ 2 Calories from Fat/ 7% Calories from Fat

Quick Sweet & Sour Dressing
½ cup peach preserves
½ cup marmalade preserves
½ cup wine vinegar
¼ teaspoon salt
⅛ teaspoon pepper

Combine the above ingredients in a blender and whip for 30 seconds. This dressing can b
in the refrigerator for a least 2 weeks.

EACH SERVING: 40 Calories/ 0 Calories from Fat/ 0% Calories from Fat

White Rice

It is very easy to make boiled rice the Chinese way, from scratch. Master this technique and you will alwa
fluffy rice. If you eat rice often, an electric rice cooker is a good investment. You are guaranteed a perfec
of rice every time.

1 cup long grain white rice
1¾ cups cold water

1. Put the rice in a 1-quart saucepan and rinse it twice with cold water. Pour off the excess water by cupping your hand over the rice grains. *Do not use a colander.* Add the cold water and bring the rice to a boil, uncovered, over high heat.

2. When the water bubbles to the top of the saucepan in about 7 minutes, turn the heat to medium and continue cooking uncovered. Stir with a fork or chopsticks occasionally to prevent sticking.

3. After about 5 minutes, when the water is almost evaporated, reduce the heat to simmer. Cover the saucepan with a tight-fitting lid and steam for about 20 minutes. Do not lift the lid during this time.

4. When the steaming is complete, fluff the rice with a fork or chopsticks. Replace the lid and let the rice stand until you are ready to serve.

PREPARATION TIME:	*2 minutes*
COOKING TIME:	*32 minutes*
YIELD:	*3½ cups cooked rice*
SERVES:	*7 (½ cup per serving)*
NOTE:	*Use the following formula to cook more rice: 2 cups of rice to 2¾ cups of water, yields 7 cups cooked rice; 3 cups of rice to 3¾ cups of water, yields about 10 cups of cooked rice. To succeed with these proportions, the rice must be rinsed twice (so that it can absorb some water) and drained by pouring the water off the rice instead of using a colander. Cup your hand over the rice as you pour off the water. Use larger saucepans for larger quantities and allow for longer cooking time.*

EACH SERVING: 113 Calories/ 0 Calories from Fat/ 0% Calories from Fat

week 3

Beef & Onions in Oyster Sauce
Stir-Tossed Potato & Carrot Sticks
Noodles with Bean Sprouts & Scallions
493 Calories/ 122 Calories from Fat/ 25% Calories from Fat

Beef & Onions in Oyster Sauce

Robust and satisfying! The oyster-flavored sauce gives this beef dish a distinctive and full-flavored taste. Your dinner guests will beg for the recipe.

8 ounces round steak, partially frozen, trimmed
1 large onion
4 large fresh mushrooms
1 tablespoon oil

MARINADE
1 teaspoon sugar
1 teaspoon cornstarch
½ teaspoon baking soda
¼ teaspoon black pepper
1 tablespoon oyster-flavored sauce
2 tablespoons dry white wine

SAUCE
½ teaspoon cornstarch
¼ teaspoon sugar
¼ teaspoon black pepper
6 tablespoons chicken broth
½ tablespoon oyster-flavored sauce
½ tablespoon lite soy sauce
1 tablespoon dry white wine

1. Cut the round steak lengthwise into slices, 1½ x ⅛ inches. Place the steak in a medium-sized bowl and set aside.

14   A WOK A WEEK

2. Blend the marinade ingredients in a small bowl until smooth and add to the beef. Toss to coat the meat well and let it stand for 30 minutes or longer.

3. Mix the ingredients for the sauce in a medium-sized bowl and set aside.

4. Cut off the ends of the onion, peel and halve it along the grain. Cut each half into ¼-inch wide slices. Set aside. Clean and thin-slice the mushrooms through the caps and stems into ¼-inch slices. Set aside.

5. When the beef has marinated for at least 30 minutes, heat a large wok on high for 30 seconds. Add the oil and swirl to coat the wok for 30 seconds. Add the onion and stir-toss for 1 minute. Add the mushrooms and cook for 30 seconds longer. Stir the sauce to be sure it is well-mixed, add it to the wok and bring the dish to a quick boil. Add the beef and marinade. Stir-toss for 3 more minutes. Ladle to a serving bowl and serve with the other hot dishes.

PREPARATION TIME: *15 minutes*
MARINATING TIME: *30 minutes or longer*
COOKING TIME: *6 minutes*
SERVES: *4*

EACH SERVING: 156 Calories/ 59 Calories from Fat/ 38% Calories from Fat

Stir-Tossed Potato & Carrot Sticks

A colorful and tasty dish to cook when fresh leafy vegetables are not available. Potatoes and carrots, stir-tossed with a touch of garlic and oyster-flavored sauce, become irresistable. Fall back on this unique and easy dish when your pantry is running low.

3 medium potatoes
2 medium carrots
1 tablespoon oil
1 teaspoon minced garlic

SEASONING
1 teaspoon sugar
½ teaspoon salt
½ teaspoon cornstarch
2 cups chicken broth
2 tablespoons oyster-flavored sauce
1 tablespoon dry white wine
4 tablespoons diced scallions

1.   Peel the potatoes and cut them into ½-inch slices. Stack 2 slices together and cut them into ¼-inch-wide strips no longer than 2 inches. Continue with the rest of the potato slices. Set them aside.

2.   Peel the carrots and slice into strips about the same size as the potatoes. Set aside.

3.   Mix the seasoning ingredients in a medium-sized bowl and set aside.

4.   Heat a wok on high for 30 seconds. Add the oil and swirl to coat the wok for 30 seconds. Add the garlic and stir-toss for 15 seconds. Add the seasoning mixture and bring it to a quick boil. Add the carrots and stir-toss for 1 minute. Add the potatoes, stir-toss, cover, and cook on medium heat for 10 minutes. Stir the vegetables occasionally to prevent sticking. Spoon to a dish and serve hot.

PREPARATION TIME: *10-12 minutes*
COOKING TIME: *15 minutes*
SERVES: *4*

EACH SERVING: 194 Calories/ 35 Calories from Fat/ 17% Calories from Fat

Noodles with Bean Sprouts & Scallions

It's hard to believe that something so simple can taste so good! I have adapted a favorite noodle dish served in *dim sum* houses and made it low-fat and still yummy. For this recipe you need to buy the special "wonton" noodles – fresh, thin noodles made with a touch of eggs. The noodles cook very quickly and are best serve *al dente*. They also come in long strands that make an ideal birthday celebration. Long noodles symbolize long life!

2 3-ounce bundles of fresh thin Chinese wonton noodles
2 quarts + 1 quart warm water from the tap
1 small onion
¼ pound fresh bean sprouts
3 large scallions
2 teaspoons sesame seed oil

SEASONING FOR NOODLES
½ tablespoon sugar
¼ teaspoon salt
2 tablespoons cider vinegar
½ tablespoon sesame seed oil
1 tablespoon Maggi seasoning

SAUCE
1 teaspoon sugar

¼ teaspoon cornstarch
¾ cup chicken broth
1½ tablespoons oyster-flavored sauce
1 tablespoon dry white wine

1. Bring 2 quarts of warm water to a rolling boil in a 4-quart saucepan. Unfold each bundle of noodles and gently place it in the boiling water. Once the noodles begin to soften, unravel the strands, so they won't stick together. Cook, uncovered for about 2 minutes – until *al dente*. Rinse quickly in a colander under cold running water. Place the noodles on a large serving platter or bowl and cut into 4-inch lengths.

2. Mix the noodle seasoning in a small bowl and add it to the noodles. Blend well, using your hands, and set aside.

3. Bring a quart of warm water to a rolling boil. Turn off heat and add the bean sprouts. Let stand for about 2 minutes. Drain and refresh in cold water. Drain again and spread bean sprouts on top of the noodles. Set aside.

4. Wash and trim the scallions. Thin-slice them lengthwise, white and greens, into slivers.

5. Trim and peel the onion. Cut it in half, and slicing with the grain, cut each half into thin slivers. Set aside.

6. In a large bowl, combine and mix the sauce ingredients until smooth. Set aside.

7. Heat a wok on high for 30 seconds. Add 1½ tablespoons of sesame seed oil and swirl to coat the wok evenly for 30 seconds. Add the onion strips and scallion slivers. Stir-toss for 1 minute. Add the sauce and bring to a quick boil. Cook for 1 more minute. Ladle sauce over the bean sprouts and noodles, toss well and serve.

PREPARATION TIME:	*8-10 minutes*
SOAKING TIME:	*2 minutes*
COOKING TIME:	*7 minutes*
SERVES:	*6 (almost a cup per serving)*

EACH SERVING: 143 Calories/ 28 Calories from Fat/ 20% Calories from Fat/

week 4

Tofu with Crab & Straw Mushrooms
Eggplant in Savory Sauce
Brown Rice
293 Calories/ 49 Calories from Fat/ 17% Calories from Fat

Tofu with Crab & Straw Mushrooms

A tofu dish that is both pretty and scrumptious. Artificial crab will do, but if you can get fresh crab, by all means, grab it up. You'll find this a superb dish you want to make often.

1 10½-ounce package of Mori-Nu lite tofu, extra-firm, drained (See note below.)
6 ounces crab
½ tablespoon oil
2 tablespoons diced scallions
1 teaspoon minced garlic
1 cup canned straw mushrooms, drained

SAUCE
½ tablespoon cornstarch
1 teaspoon sugar
¼ teaspoon salt
¼ teaspoon black pepper
¾ cup chicken broth
2 tablespoons 2% milk
2 tablespoons cold water
2 tablespoons oyster-flavored sauce

1. Drain tofu well and cut into 1 x 1 x ¼-inch thick slices. Set aside.

2. Mix the sauce ingredients in a medium-sized bowl until smooth and set aside.

3. Cut the crab into 1-inch lengths and with your fingers, separate the strands. Set aside.

4. Heat a wok on high for 30 seconds. Add oil and swirl to coat wok for 30 seconds. Add scallions and garlic. Stir-toss for 15 seconds. Add the tofu and stir-toss for 30 seconds. Mix in the sauce, stir and bring to a quick boil. Add the crab and straw mushrooms. Stir-toss and bring to a second boil. Cook for 3 more minutes. Ladle to a serving dish.

PREPARATION TIME:	10-12 minutes
COOKING TIME:	6 minutes
SERVES:	5
NOTE:	Mori-Nu lite tofu is truly low-fat – only 1% fat per serving. Other kinds of tofu have much high fat content. The extra-firm variety has more texture.

EACH SERVING: 105 Calories/ 26 Calories from Fat/ 25% Calories from Fat

Eggplant in Savory Sauce

If you have never cooked eggplant before, this recipe will make a eggplant convert of you! Simple, but luscious, this versatile recipe can be made ahead of time and reheated – or served cold.

1 large eggplant
8 medium-sized fresh mushrooms
½ cup chicken broth

SAUCE
1½ teaspoons sugar
¼ teaspoon black pepper
1 tablespoon wine vinegar
1 tablespoon lite soy sauce
1 tablespoon oyster-flavored sauce
½ tablespoon sesame seed oil
½ teaspoon minced garlic

1. Wash the eggplant but do not peel it. Cut off the top and quarter it lengthwise. Cut across each quarter to make ¼-inch-thick slices. Place the slices in a microwave-safe dish with a cover. Set aside.

2. Clean the mushrooms and trim the stems if necessary. Thin-slice through each mushroom cap and stem, making ¼-inch thick slices. Add the mushrooms to the eggplant. Pour in the broth, cover the dish, and microwave it on high for 10 minutes. Stir the vegetables, cover, and microwave on high for another 10 minutes.

3. While the dish is cooking, mix the sauce ingredients in a small covered jar and shake to blend. When the vegetables are done, add the sauce and toss the mixture with a fork until it is well-blended. Serve with the rice.

PREPARATION TIME:	*5-8 minutes*
COOKING TIME:	*20 minutes*
SERVES:	*4*
VARIATIONS:	*For a spicy Sichuan flavor, add 1 to 2 tablespoons of Hunan chili paste to the sauce.*

EACH SERVING: 72 Calories/ 18 Calories from Fat/ 25% Calories from Fat

Brown Rice

Brown rice has more bran and fiber and is also more nutritious than white rice. Its nutty taste and texture give it a distinctive appeal. The kernels need to be washed three times so they will absorb more water before cooking.

1 cup long grain brown rice
2 cups cold water

1. Place the rice in a 1-quart saucepan and rinse it three separate times with cold water. Pour off the excess water, cupping your hand over the rice grains. Do not use a colander. Add 2 cups of cold water to the rice and bring it to a boil, uncovered, over high heat.

2. When the water bubbles to the top of the saucepan, in about 10 minutes, turn the heat to medium and continue cooking uncovered. Stir the rice with chopsticks or a fork occasionally to prevent sticking.

3. After about 5 minutes when the water has almost evaporated, turn the heat to simmer. Cover the pot with a tight-fitting lid and steam for about 20 minutes. Do not lift the cover during this time.

4. When steaming is complete, fluff the rice with chopsticks. Let the rice stand, covered, until you are ready to serve.

PREPARATION TIME: *2 minutes*
COOKING TIME: *35 minutes*
YIELD: *2½ cups of cooked rice*
SERVES: *5 (½ cup per serving)*

EACH SERVING: 116 Calories/ 5 Calories from Fat/ 5% Calories from Fat

week

February

1	Steamed Turkey Meatballs Stir-Tossed Cabbage with Ginger Fragrant Rice
2	Sweet & Sour Fish Crunchy Peapods White Rice
3	Pork Chops Baked in Hoisin Sauce Bean Sprouts Fit for a King Noodles in Broth
4	Lettuce Wraps with Chicken & Mushrooms Chinese Broccoli & Straw Mushrooms Brown Rice

February week 1

Steamed Turkey Meatballs

This elegant yet simple dish is one of Donna's favorites. It serves well either as an entree or appetizer. The rice should be chilled so that it doesn't clump when you roll the turkey balls in it. Day-old rice is the easiest to work with.

12 whole canned water chestnuts
½ pound ground lean turkey
2 egg whites, lightly beaten
2½ cups cooked rice, chilled

SEASONING
½ teaspoon cornstarch
1 teaspoon sugar
½ teaspoon salt
dash of black pepper
1 tablespoon lite soy sauce
1 tablespoon dry white wine
1 teaspoon oyster-flavored sauce
1 tablespoon minced garlic
1 tablespoon diced onion

1. Fill a Chinese steamer to the halfway mark with hot water from the tap. Cover the steamer and bring the water to a rolling boil in about 10 minutes.

2. Mix the seasoning ingredients in a small bowl and set aside. Quarter the water chestnuts. Place them with the ground turkey, egg white, and seasoning mixture in a food processor. Fine-chop for 1 minute.

3. Spread the cooked rice on a large plate. Scoop out 1 teaspoon of turkey mixture, shape it into a ball and place it on the rice. Continue until all the turkey mixture is used and you have about 40 turkey meatballs. Then roll each meatball, one at a time, in the cooked rice, coating it completely. Place the meatballs on plates that fit in your steamer.

4. Put the plates of meatballs on steamer racks. When the water in the steamer has come to a rolling boil, place the steamer racks in the steamer, cover, and steam on high for 7 minutes. Do not lift the lid during steaming.

5. Serve hot. Donna even likes them cold!

PREPARATION TIME: *18-20 minutes*
COOKING TIME: *7 minutes*
SERVES: *6 as an entree; halve the recipe to serve it as an appetizer.*

EACH SERVING: 176 Calories/ 26 Calories from Fat/ 15% Calories from Fat

Stir-Tossed Cabbage with Ginger

Delicious hot or cold, this dish lifts the lowly cabbage into elegance. Ginger root heightens the flavor and reduces the gaseous nature of the cabbage.

½ head medium-sized cabbage
1 small knob gingerroot
1 small onion
6 medium mushrooms
½ tablespoon oil
½ teaspoon salt

SEASONING
1 teaspoon sugar
½ teaspoon cornstarch
1/8 teaspoon black pepper
¼ cup chicken broth
2 tablespoons water

2 tablespoons lite soy sauce
1 tablespoon dry white wine

1. Mix the seasoning ingredients in a medium-sized bowl and set aside.

2. Rinse and core the cabbage. Cut 3-inch wedges and then slice each wedge crosswise into ¼-inch-wide strips. Set aside. Smash the gingerroot to release its flavor and set aside.

3. Peel and cut off the ends of the onion. Halve and thin-slice the onion with the grain. Set aside. Clean the mushrooms, thin-slice them through the cap and stem, and set them aside.

4. Heat a wok on high for 30 seconds. Add the oil and salt and swirl to coat the wok for 30 seconds longer. Add the gingerroot and stir-toss for 30 seconds. Add the onion slices and mushrooms. Stir-toss for 1 minute. Add the cabbage and stir-toss for another minute. Add the seasoning mixture and stir-toss for 30 seconds. Cover the wok, lower the heat to medium-high and cook for 8 more minutes. Discard the gingerroot before serving.

PREPARATION TIME: *10-12 minutes*
COOKING TIME: *12 minutes*
SERVES: *4*

EACH SERVING: 72 Calories/ 20 Calories from Fat/ 27% Calories from Fat

Fragrant Rice

Using jasmine rice instead of regular long grain rice introduces a fragrance the Chinese call *Hsiang mi,* "fragrant rice." Our recipe sweetens the pot even more by adding celery, scallions and cilantro and using chicken broth instead of water.

1 cup jasmine rice
1 teaspoon oil
3 stalks of celery, diced (preferably stalks near the heart)
1½ cups chicken broth
2 tablespoons diced scallions
2 tablespoons minced cilantro or Chinese parsley
½ teaspoon freshly ground white pepper

1. Put the rice in a large bowl and rinse it twice in cold water. Pour off the excess water by cupping your hand over the rice grains. Do not use a colander. Set aside.

2. Heat a 2-quart saucepan, add the oil and swirl it for 15 seconds to coat the pan. Add the celery and stir-toss for 45 seconds. Add the chicken broth and bring it to a boil. Add the rice and bring the pot to a second boil.

Boil until the broth bubbles to the top, about 3 minutes. Turn the heat to medium and continue cooking, uncovered. Stir occasionally to prevent sticking.

3. When the broth is mostly evaporated (after about 5 minutes) reduce the heat to simmer, cover the pot with a tight-fitting lid and steam for 20 minutes more. Do not lift the lid during this time.

4. When the steaming is complete, fluff the rice, mix in the scallions, cilantro and pepper, fluff again, and serve immediately.

PREPARATION TIME: *5 minutes*
COOKING TIME: *31 minutes*
SERVES: *8 (½ cup servings)*

EACH SERVING: 99 Calories/ 8 Calories from Fat/ 9% Calories from Fat

week 2

Sweet & Sour Fish
Crunchy Peapods
White Rice
402 Calories/ 76 Calories from Fat/ 19% Calories from Fat

Sweet & Sour Fish

Poaching fish is a viable alternative to steaming and produces an equally tender texture so important to the Chinese. The poaching time may be extended to 25 or 30 minutes without damaging the texture. To cook the fish whole, you will need a Dutch oven large enough to hold the fish on a heatproof platter.

1 whole fish, head, tail and fins intact
a 1½-knob of gingerroot
2 quarts warm water
½ small cucumber
½ small sweet red pepper
½ small onion
1 tablespoon oil

SAUCE
1½ tablespoons sugar
1 teaspoon cornstarch
⅛ teaspoon black pepper
¾ cup chicken broth
3 tablespoons wine vinegar
2 tablespoons dry white wine
2 tablespoons ketchup

1. Get your Dutch oven and fish platter ready. Make sure the platter can hold the entire fish and still fit into the Dutch oven.

2. Rinse the fish and pat it dry with paper towels. Make several crosswise cuts about 1-inch apart and ½-inch deep on each side. Place the fish on the platter. Set aside.

3. Put the warm water in the Dutch oven. Smash the gingerroot flat to release its flavor. Add it to the Dutch oven and bring the water to a quick boil over high heat. Turn off the heat. Place the fish platter in the Dutch oven so that the water covers it. *Do not cover the Dutch oven.* Let the fish sit for 18 to 20 minutes. Since the heat is turned off and the pot is not covered, the fish will not overcook, even if it sits in the water for an extra 5 minutes.

4. Peel and thin-slice the onion with the grain. Thin-slice the red pepper and cucumber into match sticks. Set aside.

5. In a medium-sized bowl, blend the sauce ingredients until smooth and set aside.

6. Minutes before you are ready to serve, heat a wok on high for 30 seconds. Add the oil and swirl to coat the wok evenly for 30 seconds. Add the onion. Stir-toss for 30 seconds. Add the red pepper and cucumber sticks. Stir-toss for 30 seconds longer. Add the sauce and bring to a quick boil. Set aside.

7. Carefully pour off the poaching liquid and gently remove the fish from the plate using slotted spatulas. Drain it well. Turn the fish bottom side up as you place it on the serving platter.

8. Ladle the sweet and sour sauce over it and serve immediately.

PREPARATION TIME:	*8-10 minutes*
POACHING TIME:	*18-20 minutes*
SERVES:	*4*
EQUIPMENT:	*A Dutch oven, a large heatproof platter, and two slotted spatulas – the longer the better.*
NOTE:	*Pickerel, whitefish and bass are delicious prepared this way.*

EACH SERVING: 219 Calories/ 60 Calories from Fat/ 28% Calories from Fat

Crunchy Peapods

The delicate flavor and wonderful crunch of Chinese peapods are enhanced by this delicious dressing. Freshness is paramount: pick firm and unblemished pods and serve this recipe chilled.

1 pound fresh Chinese peapods
1 cup water

DRESSING
1½ teaspoons sugar
½ teaspoon salt
⅛ teaspoon black pepper
1 tablespoon lite soy sauce
½ tablespoon sesame seed oil
1 teaspoon minced garlic

1. Mix the dressing ingredients in a small bowl and set aside.

2. Wash and snip off the top of each peapod. Place the peapods in a large microwave-safe dish and add the cup of water. Cover and microwave on high for 2½ minutes. Drain the peapods and refresh them in cold water to stop the cooking. Pat them dry.

3. Pour the dressing over the peapods and toss to mix well. Serve immediately or chill and serve.

PREPARATION TIME:	*8-10 minutes*
COOKING TIME:	*2½ minutes*
CHILLING TIME:	*30 minutes*
SERVES	*4*
MAKE AHEAD:	*Yes*

EACH SERVING: 70 Calories/ 16 Calories from Fat/ 23% Calories from Fat

White Rice

It is very easy to make boiled rice the Chinese way, from scratch. Master this technique and you will always enjoy fluffy rice. If you eat rice often, an electric rice cooker is a good investment. You are guaranteed a perfect pot of rice every time.

1 cup long grain white rice
1¾ cups cold water

1. Put the rice in a 1-quart saucepan and rinse it twice with cold water. Pour off the excess water by cupping your hand over the rice grains. *Do not use a colander.* Add the cold water and bring the rice to a boil, uncovered, over high heat.

2. When the water bubbles to the top of the saucepan in about 7 minutes, turn the heat to medium and continue cooking uncovered. Stir with a fork or chopsticks occasionally to prevent sticking.

3. After about 5 minutes, when the water is almost evaporated, reduce the heat to simmer. Cover the saucepan with a tight-fitting lid and steam for about 20 minutes. Do not lift the lid during this time.

4. When the steaming is complete, fluff the rice with a fork or chopsticks. Replace the lid and let the rice stand until you are ready to serve.

PREPARATION TIME:	*2 minutes*
COOKING TIME:	*32 minutes*
YIELD:	*3½ cups cooked rice*
SERVES:	*7 (½ cup per serving)*
NOTE:	*Use the following formula to cook more rice: 2 cups of rice to 2¾ cups of water, yields 7 cups cooked rice; 3 cups of rice to 3¾ cups of water, yields about 10 cups of cooked rice. To succeed with these proportions, the rice must be rinsed twice (so that it can absorb some water) and drained by pouring the water off the rice instead of using a calender. Cup your hand over the rice as you pour off the water. Use a larger saucepan for larger quantities and allow for longer cooking time.*

EACH SERVING: 113 Calories/ 0 Calories from Fat/ 0% Calories from Fat

week 3

Pork Chops Baked in Hoisin Sauce
Bean Sprouts Fit for a King
Noodles in Broth
355 Calories/ 82 Calories from Fat/ 23% Calories from Fat

Pork Chops Baked in Hoisin Sauce

A dish that is both rich and elegant. Hoisin sauce and 5-spice powder marry well and together add zest and fragrance to the chops.

4 boneless center cut pork chops, very lean
2 large scallions, diced
1 cup chicken broth

MARINADE
1 teaspoon cornstarch
½ teaspoon 5-spice powder
¼ teaspoon baking soda
¼ teaspoon black pepper
3 tablespoons hoisin sauce
2 tablespoons cold water
1 tablespoon whiskey
1 tablespoon honey
½ tablespoon oyster-flavored sauce
½ teaspoon minced garlic

1. Trim all fat from the pork chops. Rinse and pat them dry with paper towels. Place the chops in a baking dish with sides and enough space so they do not overlap.

2. Mix the marinade and add it to the chops. Marinate for 30 minutes or longer. Turning the chops occasionally will ensure that both sides are well coated with the marinade.

3. Preheat the oven to 375 degrees.

4. Just before baking, add the diced scallions and chicken broth to the chops, mixing them in with the marinade. Bake the chops on a mid-oven rack for 10 minutes. Turn, baste, and bake them for another 10 minutes.

5. Ladle the chops and sauce onto a platter. Serve right away.

PREPARATION TIME:	*12-15 minutes*
MARINATING TIME:	*30 minutes*
COOKING TIME:	*20 minutes*
SERVES:	*4*
NOTE:	*Dry white wine may be substituted for the whiskey, but the dish is not as tasty. Try marinating the chops overnight for an even tastier flavor.*

EACH SERVING: 195 Calories/ 58 Calories from Fat/ 30% Calories from Fat

Bean Sprouts Fit for a King

The tangy taste of peppers, garlic and scallions turns "lowly" bean sprouts into a dish fit for a king. For a even greater visual treat, try using a kaleidoscopic combination of red, yellow and green peppers.

1 pound fresh bean sprouts
1 large green pepper
2 scallions with green tops
½ tablespoon oil
1 teaspoon minced garlic
1 tablespoon Maggi seasoning

SEASONING
1 teaspoon sugar
½ teaspoon salt
½ teaspoon cornstarch
⅛ teaspoon freshly ground white pepper
½ cup chicken broth
1 tablespoon dry white wine

1. Wash and drain the bean sprouts. Set them aside. Wash and halve the green pepper. Cut off and discard top, core and seeds. Cut each half into 3 pieces, lengthwise. Thin-slice each length crosswise into ⅛-inch wide pieces. Set aside.

2. Trim the roots off the scallions. Wash, pat dry, and cut them diagonally into fine slivers .

3. Mix seasoning ingredients in a small bowl and set aside.

4. Heat a wok on high for 30 seconds. Add the oil and swirl to coat the wok for 30 seconds longer. Add the minced garlic and stir-toss for 15 seconds. Add the seasoning mixture and bring it to a boil. Add the green pepper strips and stir-toss for 30 seconds. Add the bean sprouts, stir-toss, and cook for 1 minute. Add the scallions, cover, and cook for 1 minute. Uncover, stir-toss, cover, and cook for another minute.

5. *Just before dishing up,* add the Maggi seasoning, mixing it well with the vegetables. Ladle to a dish and serve hot.

PREPARATION TIME:	*6-8 minutes*
COOKING TIME:	*6 minutes*
SERVES:	*6*
NOTE:	*For a totally vegetarian presentation, use vegetable broth.*

EACH SERVING: 58 Calories/ 14 Calories from Fat/ 23% Calories from Fat

Noodles in Broth

Whenever I need comfort on a cold winter night, this is the noodle dish I crave. Try it with spinach, bok choy, Napa cabbage or any of your favorite leafy greens. Please note that this is *not a soup to be served before meals*, but a noodle dish to be eaten *with your entree*.

¼ pound thin, dry noodles or vermicelli
8 cups cold water
10 ounces chopped spinach, fresh or frozen
4 cups chicken broth

1. Bring the water to a rolling boil in a 4-quart covered saucepan. Add the noodles and cook them uncovered for about 7 minutes – until they are tender to the bite.

2. While the noodles cook, bring the chicken broth to boil in a large, covered pot. Add the spinach and bring to a second boil. Remove from the heat, cover, and set aside.

3. When the noodles are done, drain and rinse them in cold water. Add them to the chicken broth pot, return the pot to the heat, and cook for 2 minutes.

4. Ladle to individual bowls and serve with the entree.

PREPARATION TIME: *Less than 5 minutes*
COOKING TIME: *24 minutes*
SERVES: *6*

EACH SERVING: 102 Calories/ 10 Calories from Fat/ 9% Calories from Fat

week 4

Lettuce Wraps with Chicken & Mushrooms
Chinese Broccoli & Straw Mushrooms
Brown Rice
301 Calories/ 46 Calories from Fat/ 15% Calories from Fat

Lettuce Wraps with Chicken & Mushrooms

Futuristic food! Fun to prepare and eat. Full of flavor and fiber. Note that the recipe calls for *cooked* chicken. Add time for steaming a chicken breast, if you don't have cooked chicken on hand.

8 large lettuce leaves, preferably bib, but romaine or iceberg will do
2 quarts cold water with 1 cup ice cubes
1 cup cooked chicken
8 medium mushrooms
3 cups alfalfa sprouts
2 ounces fat-free mozzarella cheese, grated

DRESSING
½ teaspoon sugar
½ teaspoon salt
¼ teaspoon black pepper
¼ cup low-fat yogurt
½ tablespoon sesame seed oil
1 tablespoon lite soy sauce
1 teaspoon Dijon mustard

1. Soak the lettuce in the ice water for 15 minutes. Drain well and set aside.

2. While the lettuce is soaking, tear or cut the cooked chicken into thin slivers. Set aside in a medium-sized bowl.

3. Mix the dressing ingredients in a small covered jar and shake to blend. Pour the dressing over the chicken and mix well.

4. Clean and thin-slice the mushrooms through the cap and stem. Arrange the lettuce leaves, chicken, sliced mushrooms, alfalfa sprouts, and grated mozzarella cheese on a large platter or on separate plates.

5. Diners make their own "finger sandwich" by placing chicken, alfalfa sprouts, mushrooms, and grated mozzarella on a lettuce leaf and roll-wrapping it. They are scrumptious. Roll, wrap, and enjoy!

PREPARATION TIME: *12-15 minutes*
COOKING TIME: *20 minutes – if you don't already have cooked chicken, otherwise zero.*
SERVES: *4 as an entree, 8 as an appetizer*

EACH WRAP: 105 Calories/ 28 Calories from Fat/ 26% Calories from Fat

Chinese Broccoli & Straw Mushrooms

The Chinese love their greens – especially Chinese broccoli or *gai lan*. *Gai lan* is prized for its taste and crunchy texture. This classic dish, served at the best Chinese restaurants and roadside stands, is one of my favorites. Use the stalks – they are tender and tasty – as well as the leaves.

1½ pounds fresh Chinese broccoli
2 quarts of warm water
a 1-inch knob of gingerroot, smashed
2 tablespoons dry white wine
1 teaspoon sugar
1 8-ounce can tiny peeled straw mushrooms, drained

SAUCE
½ teaspoon sugar
½ teaspoon cornstarch
¼ cup chicken broth
2 tablespoons water from the mushrooms
2 tablespoons oyster-flavored sauce
½ tablespoon sesame seed oil

1. Bring the warm water, wine, sugar and gingerroot to a quick boil in a 6-quart covered saucepan.

2. Rinse and drain the *gai lan* without cutting or breaking the stalks and leaves. Set aside.

3. When the water comes to a boil, add the *gai lan* and cook, uncovered, for 4 to 5 minutes – until it turns bright, vibrant green. Drain and arrange artistically on a large platter.

4. While the *gai lan* is cooking, mix the sauce ingredients in a large bowl, and add the straw mushrooms. Microwave on high for 2 minutes and then pour over the *gai lan*.

Delicious hot or cold.

PREPARATION TIME:	*Less than 5 minutes*
COOKING TIME:	*12 minutes*
MAKE AHEAD:	*Yes, serve cold.*
SERVES:	*6*

EACH SERVING: 80 Calories/ 13 Calories from Fat/ 16% Calories from Fat

Brown Rice

Brown rice has more bran and fiber and is also more nutritious than white rice. Its nutty taste and texture give it a distinctive appeal. The kernels need to be washed three times so they will absorb more water before cooking.

1 cup long grain brown rice
2 cups cold water

1. Place the rice in a 1-quart saucepan and rinse it three separate times with cold water. Pour off the excess water, cupping your hand over the rice grains. Do not use a colander. Add 2 cups of cold water to the rice and bring it to a boil, uncovered, over high heat.

2. When the water bubbles to the top of the saucepan, in about 10 minutes, turn the heat to medium and continue cooking uncovered. Stir the rice with chopsticks or a fork occasionally to prevent sticking.

3. After about 5 minutes when the water has almost evaporated, turn the heat to simmer. Cover the pot with a tight-fitting lid and steam for about 20 minutes. Do not lift the cover during this time.

4. When steaming is complete, fluff the rice with chopsticks. Let the rice stand, covered, until you are ready to serve.

PREPARATION TIME:	*2 minutes*
COOKING TIME:	*35 minutes*
YIELD:	*2½ cups of cooked rice*
SERVES:	*5 (½ cup per serving)*

EACH SERVING: 116 Calories/ 5 Calories from Fat/ 5% Calories from Fat

week

March

1
Sichuan Chicken
Green Bean & Water Chestnut Salad
Sesame Noodles

2
Poached Fish Fillets with Ginger & Scallions
Ivory & Jade Flowers
White Rice

3
Cucumber Soup
Meatballs in Hot & Spicy Sauce
Rice with Spinach & Carrots

4
Braised Lamb with Leeks
Asparagus Spears
Brown Rice

March week 1

Sichuan Chicken
Green Bean & Water Chestnut Salad
Sesame Noodles
334 Calories/ 76 Calories from Fat/ 23% Calories from Fat

Sichuan Chicken

Delicious baked or grilled, this spicy, plan-ahead dish is well worth the 2-hour marinating time.

4 *4-ounce chicken thighs, skinned and boned*
     OR
2 *8-ounce chicken breasts, skinned and boned*

MARINADE
2 teaspoons sugar
1 teaspoon cornstarch
¼ teaspoon baking soda
¼ teaspoon black pepper
1½ cups cold water
2 tablespoons dry white wine
1½ tablespoons Hunan chili paste
1½ tablespoons oyster-flavored sauce
2 tablespoons scallions, diced
1 teaspoon garlic, minced
½ teaspoon gingerroot, grated

1. Wash the chicken, remove all fat, pat dry with paper towels. Set aside.

2. In a large bowl, mix the marinade and add the chicken. Refrigerate for two hours or more. Turn the meat occasionally to assure that the seasoning penetrates all the flesh.

3. When the chicken is almost through marinating, preheat the oven to 375 degrees. Line a baking pan with foil and put the chicken and its marinade in it. Bake for 25 minutes; turn it over and continue baking for another 20 minutes. Baste the chicken as you turn it.

4. Remove the chicken to a serving platter and top with any sauce left in the baking pan. Serve hot.

PREPARATION TIME: *12 minutes*
MARINATING TIME: *2 hours*
COOKING TIME: *45 minutes*
SERVES: *4*
NOTE: *Use more or less Hunan chili paste to make the dish more or less spicy: fiery hot is 2 to 3 tablespoons; medium hot, 1 to 1½; and mild, ½ to ¾. Different brands also vary in intensity. Experiment for best results – and remember, it is much easier to add more chili paste than it is to cook more noodles, so begin with a mild mix!*

*EACH SERVING WITH **WHITE** MEAT:*
159 Calories/ 14 Calories from Fat/9% Calories from Fat

*EACH SERVING WITH **DARK** MEAT:*
139 Calories/ 31 Calories from Fat/ 23% Calories from Fat

Green Bean & Water Chestnut Salad

What could be more appealing than this salad when green beans are in season? Coupled with thinly-sliced, crunchy water chestnuts, this dish is also a treat for the eyes.

1 pound fresh green beans
1 cup water
1 11-ounce can sliced water chestnuts
1 teaspoon minced garlic

DRESSING
1 teaspoon sugar
½ teaspoon salt
⅛ teaspoon black pepper
1 tablespoon water
1 tablespoon lite soy sauce
1 tablespoon oyster-flavored sauce
½ tablespoon sesame seed oil

1. Mix the dressing ingredients in a small bowl and set aside.

2. Wash the green beans and snip off the ends. Place them in a large microwave-safe bowl, add the water, cover and microwave on high for 9 minutes. Drain and refresh the beans with cold water to stop the cooking. Pat them dry.

3. Add the dressing and stir thoroughly to coat the beans. Add the sliced water chestnuts and minced garlic. Toss again to blend well and serve.

PREPARATION TIME: *8-10 minutes*
COOKING TIME: *9 minutes*
SERVES: *4*
MAKE AHEAD: *Yes, serve chilled.*

EACH SERVING: 83 Calories/ 16 Calories from Fat/ 19% Calories from Fat

Sesame Noodles

My low-calorie version of a traditional Beijing favorite. Roadside stands and fine restaurants alike boast of their special sesame noodles recipes. Try mine!

2 quarts cold water
¼ pound thin dry noodles or vermicelli
1 large scallion
1 small carrot
1 tablespoon water
1 tablespoon toasted sesame seeds

DRESSING
½ teaspoon sugar
¼ teaspoon salt
¼ teaspoon black pepper
1 tablespoon cider vinegar
1 tablespoon lite soy sauce
1 tablespoon sesame seed oil
1 teaspoon minced garlic

1. Bring 2 quarts of water to a rolling boil in a 4-quart saucepan. Add the vermicelli and cook, uncovered, for about 7 minutes – until they are tender to the bite.

2. While the noodles are cooking, fine-cut the carrot. Place the carrot slivers in a microwave-safe dish with 1 tablespoon of cold water and cook, covered, on high for 1 minute. Pour out the water and set the carrots aside. Fine-cut the scallion into slivers and set aside.

3. Drain the noodles in a colander under cold running water. Transfer them to a large bowl. Blend the dressing ingredients by shaking them in a small covered jar and pour this mixture over the noodles. Mix well, then add the toasted sesame seeds (see note below) and mix again. Garnish with the scallion and carrot slivers. Delicious hot or cold.

PREPARATION TIME:	*5-10 minutes*
COOKING TIME:	*12-15 minutes*
YIELD:	*3 cups cooked noodles*
SERVES:	*6 (½ cup per serving)*
NOTE:	*Sesame seeds need to be toasted to bring out their sweet, nutlike flavor. Spread the seeds on a cookie sheet and bake them for 30 minutes in a 250-degree oven. Toasted seeds can be stored in an airtight covered jar for weeks – ready to use in other dishes.*
MAKE AHEAD:	*Yes, serve chilled.*

EACH SERVING: 112 Calories/ 29 Calories from Fat/ 26% Calories from Fat

week 2

Poached Fish Fillet with Ginger & Scallions
Ivory & Jade Flowers
White Rice
325 Calories/ 58 Calories from Fat/ 18% Calories from Fat

Poached Fish Fillets with Ginger & Scallions

Amazingly simple to prepare and yet incredibly delicious, this dish must be tried to be believed! Here's a little secret: pick the freshest fish you can find. Whether you use whitefish, salmon, pickerel, snapper, or scrod – your family will be delighted with this treat.

1 pound fresh fish fillet
2 quarts warm water
a 1-inch knob gingerroot

SAUCE
1 tablespoon oil
4 thin slices gingerroot, slivered
2 scallions with greens, slivered
2 tablespoons Maggie seasoning

1. Crush the ginger knob to release its full flavor. Add it to the warm water in a 4-quart pot and bring to a quick boil.

2. Rinse the fillet and pat it dry with paper towels. Cut it lengthwise into four pieces and set them aside.

3. Cut the scallions and gingerroot slices into thin slivers and set them aside.

4. When the ginger water comes to a boil, turn off the heat and add the fillet sections. Poach for about 3 minutes. Check to see if the fish has turned opaque and flakes easily. If some of the flesh is still transparent, poach for another minute. With a slotted spatula gently lift each section from the water, drain it well, and place it on a serving platter. Set the platter aside.

5. Heat the oil in a small saucepan. When it starts to smoke, turn off the heat and add the scallions and gingerroot. Stir-toss for 30 seconds. Add the Maggie seasoning. Stir, then spread the sauce over the fish. Serve immediately.

PREPARATION TIME:	*6 to 8 minutes*
COOKING TIME:	*10 to 11 minutes*
SERVES:	*4*

EACH SERVING: 138 Calories/ 38 Calories from Fat/ 29% Calories from Fat

Ivory & Jade Flowers

Stir-tossed and flavored with garlic and oyster sauce, these vegetables are simply scrumptious. This is one of Donna's favorite recipes. Try to stop at just one helping.

½ large head cauliflower
1 stalk broccoli
½ tablespoon oil
1 teaspoon minced garlic
½ teaspoon salt

SEASONING
1 teaspoon sugar

½ teaspoon cornstarch
¼ teaspoon black pepper
2 tablespoons chicken broth
2 tablespoons water
1 tablespoon oyster-flavored sauce
1 tablespoon dry white wine

1. Rinse the cauliflower. Remove and discard the leaves and cut off about 1 inch of the stem. Separate flowerets and cut them into 2-inch long pieces. Half or quarter the thicker pieces.

2. Rinse the broccoli and cut the flowerets into 2-inch lengths. Peel the broccoli stalk with a paring knife. Slice the stalk into ½-inch diagonal slices or roll-cut it into 2-inch lengths. Set aside.

3. Mix the seasoning ingredients in a medium-sized bowl and set aside.

4. Heat a wok on high for 30 seconds. Add the oil and swirl to coat the wok for 30 seconds longer. Add the garlic and salt. Stir-toss for 15 seconds. Add the cauliflower. Stir-toss for 1 minute. Add the broccoli and stir-toss for 1 more minute. Pour in the seasoning mixture, blend well, cover, and cook for 3 minutes longer. This dish may be served hot or cold.

PREPARATION TIME: *8-10 minutes*
COOKING TIME: *7 minutes*
SERVES: *4*

EACH SERVING: 74 Calories/ 20 Calories from Fat/ 25% Calories from Fat

White Rice

It is very easy to make boiled rice the Chinese way, from scratch. Master this technique and you will always enjoy fluffy rice. If you eat rice often, an electric rice cooker is a good investment. You are guaranteed a perfect pot of rice every time.

1 cup long grain white rice
1¾ cups cold water

1. Put the rice in a 1-quart saucepan and rinse it twice with cold water. Scoop off the excess water by cupping your hand over the rice grains. *Do not use a colander.* Add the cold water and bring the rice to a boil, uncovered, over high heat.

2. When the water bubbles to the top of the saucepan in about 7 minutes, turn the heat to medium and continue cooking uncovered. Stir with a fork or chopsticks occasionally to prevent sticking.

3. After about 5 minutes, when the water is almost evaporated, reduce the heat to simmer. Cover the saucepan with a tight-fitting lid and steam for about 20 minutes. Do not lift the lid during this time.

4. When the steaming is complete, fluff the rice once again with a fork or chopsticks. Replace the lid and let the rice stand until you are ready to serve.

PREPARATION TIME:	*2 minutes*
COOKING TIME:	*32 minutes*
YIELD:	*3½ cups cooked rice*
SERVES:	*7 (½ cup per serving)*
NOTE:	*Use the following formula to cook more rice: 2 cups of rice to 2¾ cups of water, yields 7 cups cooked rice; 3 cups of rice to 3¾ cups of water, yields about 10 cups of cooked rice. To succeed with these proportions, the rice must be rinsed twice and drained by cupping your hand over the rice grains. Use larger saucepots for larger quantities and allow for longer cooking time.*

EACH SERVING: 113 Calories/ 0 Calories from Fat/ 0% Calories from Fat

week 3

Cucumber Soup
Meatballs in Hot & Spicy Sauce
Rice with Spinach & Carrots
328 Calories/ 62 Calories from Fat/ 19% Calories from Fat

Cucumber Soup

Nothing could be simpler or more appealing than this light and refreshing soup. Fun to make and serve to your favorite guests.

1 small cucumber
1 small carrot
4 large mushrooms
4 cups chicken broth
2 egg whites, lightly beaten

GARNISH
1 tablespoon diced scallions

1. Put the broth in a 2-quart saucepan and bring it to a boil over high heat. While it is cooking, prepare the vegetables.

2. Clean and trim the carrot. Thin-slice it into rounds and set them aside.

3. Wash and peel the cucumber, cutting off both ends. Quarter it lengthwise. Thin-slice each quarter, crosswise, and set aside.

4. Clean and thin-slice the mushrooms, cutting across the cap and stem. Set aside.

5. When the broth comes to a boil, add the carrot slices and turn the heat to medium. Cook, covered, for 5 minutes. Add the cucumber and mushroom slices, cover and continue to cook for 5 more minutes.

6. Turn off the heat and drizzle in egg whites in a thin stream. Add salt and pepper to taste and ladle into individual soup bowls. Garnish with diced scallions and serve.

PREPARATION TIME: *8-10 minutes*
COOKING TIME: *17 minutes*
SERVES: *4*

EACH SERVING: 57 Calories/ 11 Calories from Fat/ 20% Calories from Fat

Meatballs in Hot & Spicy Sauce

An easy-to-make dish for those who have a taste for the hot and spicy. This versatile recipe serves well as an appetizer or an entree.

1 pound very lean ground sirloin

SEASONING
1½ tablespoons cornstarch
1 teaspoon sugar
¼ teaspoon baking soda
¼ teaspoon black pepper
½ tablespoon lite soy sauce
1 tablespoon dry white wine
½ tablespoon oyster-flavored sauce
1 tablespoon cold water
1 small onion, finely minced

HOT & SPICY SAUCE
½ tablespoon cornstarch
1½ teaspoons sugar
1 cup cold water
2 tablespoons Hunan chili paste
2 tablespoons oyster-flavored sauce
2 tablespoons ketchup

1. In a large bowl, blend the seasoning ingredients until smooth. Add the ground beef and mix well. Let stand for 30 minutes or longer. Knead the mixture for 1 minute. Roll the meat into 1-inch balls. Repeat until you use all the meat. You should have 35 to 40 meatballs. Set aside. Wetting your hands from time to time will help you make smoother meatballs.

2. Mix ingredients for the hot and spicy sauce in a medium bowl and set aside.

3. Heat a wok on high for 30 seconds. Add the hot and spicy sauce and bring it to a boil. Turn the heat to medium and add the meatballs. Cover and cook for 3 minutes. Roll the meatballs over gently with a spatula and cook for another 3 minutes. Remove the meatballs and sauce to a serving dish. Serve piping hot.

PREPARATION TIME:	*25-30 minutes*
MARINATING TIME:	*30 minutes*
COOKING TIME:	*8 minutes*
SERVES:	*5*
NOTE:	*Adjust the amount of Hunan chili paste to suit your taste. Different brands also vary in intensity. Experiment for best results.*

EACH SERVING: 167 Calories/ 43 Calories from Fat/ 26 % Calories from Fat

Rice with Spinach & Carrots

Once I tasted this dish at a fancy restaurant in San Antonio, I knew I had to include my version of it in my next collection. Steamed rice comes alive with chopped spinach and grated carrots.

½ cup rice
½ cup cold water
6 tablespoons chicken broth
2½ ounces chopped spinach, fresh or frozen (defrosted and drained)
½ small carrot, coarsely grated
salt to taste

SEASONING
¼ teaspoon sugar
dash of black pepper
½ teaspoon sesame seed oil

1. Place the rice in a 2-quart saucepan and rinse it twice with cold water. To drain, pour off the excess water, cupping your hand over the grains. *Do not use a colander.* Add the fresh cold water, chicken broth, spinach and grated carrot. Bring the rice to a boil, uncovered, over high heat.

2. When the water bubbles to the top of the saucepan, in about 8 minutes, reduce the heat to simmer. Cover the pot with a tight-fitting lid and steam, without lifting the lid, for 20 minutes. Check to see if all the liquid has been absorbed. If not, continue steaming for a few minutes more.

3. When the rice is done, remove it from the heat, fluff it, replace the cover and let it stand until the other dishes are ready.

4. Just before serving, mix the seasoning and add it to the rice. Blend well and add salt if you wish. Serve immediately.

PREPARATION TIME:	*5 minutes*
COOKING TIME:	*33 minutes*
SERVES:	*4 (½ cup servings)*
NOTE:	*If you are using an automatic rice cooker, follow the same process. Add the spinach and carrot to the rice before steaming; add the seasoning when the rice is done and you are ready to serve it.*

EACH SERVING: 104 Calories/ 8 Calories from Fat/ 7% Calories from Fat

week 4

Braised Lamb with Leeks
Asparagus Spears
Brown Rice
372 Calories/ 71 Calories from Fat/ 19% Calories from Fat

Braised Lamb with Leeks

An easy and delicious way to cook lamb shanks – a favorite among the people of northern China. Leeks add the special dimension to this dish. Small lamb shanks weighing no more than ½ pound each are preferred. If these are not easy to find, 2 larger ones weighing a pound each will do. I usually like to cook this dish a day or two ahead, allowing the flavor to mellow.

4 8-ounce or 2 1-pound lamb shanks
1 whole leek
a 1-inch knob of gingerroot
½ tablespoon oil

MARINADE
2 tablespoons lite soy sauce
2 tablespoons whiskey

SEASONING
1 tablespoon sugar
¼ teaspoon black pepper
3 cups cold water
½ cup dry white wine
2 tablespoons oyster-flavored sauce
2 tablespoons cider vinegar

1. Mix the marinade ingredients in a large bowl, big enough for the shanks.

2. Rinse the shanks and pat them dry with paper towels. Add them to the marinade. Let stand for 30 minutes or longer, turning occasionally.

3. Trim the roots from the leek. Cut it in two where the white stem turns green. Cut the stem in two, lengthwise. Fan out the leaves and wash both the green and white parts carefully. (Dirt usually hides in the green stalk.) Cut each strip – greens and bulb – in half, lenghwise, once again. Finally, cut those strips into 1-inch pieces. Set aside.

4. Smash the gingerroot flat to release its full flavor. Set aside.

5. In a large bowl blend the sauce ingredients until smooth and set aside.

6. After the lamb has marinated for at least 30 minutes, heat a 6-quart saucepan for 30 seconds. Add the oil and swirl to coat the bottom of the saucepan for 30 seconds. Add the gingerroot and stir-toss for 10 seconds. Add the leeks. Stir-toss for about 1 minute. Add the lamb shanks *but reserve the marinade*. Brown both sides for about 1 minute a side. Add the marinade and seasoning and bring to a boil. Turn heat to low, cover, and let it simmer for 2 hours.

7. The meat will be so tender it will fall off the bones. Remove the bones, return the meat to the sauce, mix well, dish up and serve.

PREPARATION TIME:	*6-8 minutes*
MARINATING TIME:	*30 minutes*
COOKING TIME:	*2 hours and 6 minutes*
SERVES:	*6*
NOTE:	*This dish can be cooked several days ahead and reheated before serving.*

EACH SERVING: 210 Calories/ 53 Calories from Fat/ 26% Calories from Fat

Asparagus Spears

A quick and simple way to serve asparagus at its best. Pick firm and unblemished spears. Take advantage of the lower prices when asparagus is in season and serve this dish often.

1½ pounds fresh asparagus spears
¼ cup chicken broth
2 teaspoons minced garlic

DRESSING
1 teaspoon sugar
¼ teaspoon black pepper
2 tablespoons lite soy sauce
½ teaspoon sesame seed oil

1. Snap off and discard the tough end of each asparagus spear. (If you bend the stalk using both hands, they will usually break at the woody part of the stem.) Wash and drain the spears. Place them in a microwave-safe dish. Add the chicken broth and garlic.

2. Cover the dish and microwave on high for 3 minutes. Pour off the liquid. Mix the dressing ingredients in a small cup and add to the cooked asparagus. Blend carefully but well.

3. This dish is delicious hot or cold. To chill for serving, refrigerate for at least ½ hour.

PREPARATION TIME:	*5 minutes*
COOKING TIME:	*3 minutes*
CHILLING TIME:	*30 minutes (optional)*
SERVES:	*4*
MAKE AHEAD:	*Yes, serve chilled.*

EACH SERVING: 46 Calories/ 13 Calories from Fat/ 26% Calories from Fat

Brown Rice

Brown rice has more bran and fiber and is also more nutritious than white rice. Its nutty taste and texture give it a distinctive appeal. The kernels need to be washed three times so they will absorb more water before cooking.

1 cup long grain brown rice
2 cups cold water

1. Place the rice in a 1-quart saucepan and rinse it three separate times with cold water. Pour off the excess water, cupping your hand over the rice grains. Do not use a colander. Add 2 cups of cold water to the rice and bring it to a boil, uncovered, over high heat.

2. When the water bubbles to the top of the saucepan, in about 10 minutes, turn the heat to medium and continue cooking uncovered. Stir the rice with chopsticks or a fork occasionally to prevent sticking.

3. After about 5 minutes when the water has almost evaporated, turn the heat to simmer. Cover the pot with a tight-fitting lid and steam for about 20 minutes. Do not lift the cover during this time.

4. When steaming is complete, fluff the rice with chopsticks. Let the rice stand, covered, until you are ready to serve.

PREPARATION TIME: *2 minutes*
COOKING TIME: *35 minutes*
YIELD: *2½ cups of cooked rice*
SERVES: *5 (½ cup per serving)*

EACH SERVING: 116 Calories/ 5 Calories from Fat/ 5% Calories from Fat

week

1
Chinese Turkey Patties
Stir-Tossed Potato & Carrot Sticks
Sichuan Noodles

2
Sweet & Sour Shrimp
Spinach & Mushrooms with Garlic
Sesame Noodles

3
Roasted Pork Chops
Asparagus with Lotus Root
Brown Rice

4
Tomato & Glassy Noodle Soup
Tofu Salad with Shrimp
White Rice

week 1

Chinese Turkey Patties
Stir-Tossed Potato & Carrot Sticks
Sichuan Noodles
413 Calories/ 69 Calories from Fat/ 17% Calories from Fat

Chinese Turkey Patties

This recipe offers a healthy and tasty alternative to beef hamburgers. The turkey patties, after a 30-minute marinating, can be broiled in a conventional oven, microwaved or grilled.

1 pound lean ground turkey
1 medium onion, diced
vegetable spray

SEASONING
1 tablespoon cornstarch
1 teaspoon sugar
½ teaspoon salt
¼ teaspoon black pepper
2 tablespoons cold water
1½ tablespoons oyster-flavored sauce
1 tablespoon whiskey
1 teaspoon minced garlic

1. In a large bowl, mix the seasoning ingredients until smooth. Add the ground turkey. Mix well and let stand for 30 minutes or longer.

2. Put the diced onion in a food processor and fine-chop for about 30 seconds, scraping down the sides occasionally with a rubber spatula. Add it to the turkey and mix well.

3. Preheat the oven on broil. Line a baking pan with aluminum foil. Coat the lined pan with a thin layer of nonfat vegetable spray and set aside.

4. After the turkey has seasoned for 30 minutes, scoop up ½ cup, shape it into a ball, then flatten it into a patty. Make four more patties. Place the turkey patties on the baking pan and the pan on the top oven rack.

5. Broil for 8 minutes. Turn the patties and broil for another 8 minutes. Serve with the noodles and vegetable.

PREPARATION TIME:	*8-10 minutes*
MARINATING TIME:	*30 minutes*
COOKING TIME:	*16 minutes*
SERVES:	*5*
VARIATION:	*Use the mixture to make 1-inch meatballs and broil them for 10 minutes. These little fellows make a great entree or delicious appetizers.*
NOTE:	*To microwave the patties, place them on a microwave-safe plate, cover with paper towels and cook on high for 5 to 6 minutes. To grill the patties, cook for about 4 to 5 minutes on each side.*

EACH SERVING: 128 Calories/ 21 Calories from Fat/ 17% Calories from Fat

Stir-Tossed Potato & Carrot Sticks

A colorful and tasty dish to cook when fresh leafy vegetables are not available. Potatoes and carrots, stir-tossed with a touch of garlic and oyster-flavored sauce, become irresistable. Fall back on this unique and easy dish when your pantry is running low.

3 medium potatoes
2 medium carrots
1 tablespoon oil
1 teaspoon minced garlic

SEASONING
1 teaspoon sugar
½ teaspoon salt
½ teaspoon cornstarch
2 cups chicken broth
2 tablespoons oyster-flavored sauce
1 tablespoon dry white wine
4 tablespoons diced scallions

1. Peel the potatoes and cut them into ½-inch slices. Stack 2 slices together and cut them into ¼-inch-wide strips no longer than 2 inches. Continue with the rest of the potato slices. Set them aside.

2. Peel the carrots and slice into strips about the same size as the potatoes. Set aside.

3. Mix the seasoning ingredients in a medium-sized bowl and set it aside.

4. Heat a wok on high for 30 seconds. Add the oil and swirl to coat the wok for 30 seconds longer. Add the garlic and stir-toss for 15 seconds. Add the seasoning mixture and bring it to a quick boil. Add the carrots and stir-toss for 1 minute. Add the potatoes, stir-toss, cover, and cook on medium heat for 10 minutes. Stir the vegetables occasionally to prevent sticking. Spoon to a dish and serve hot.

PREPARATION TIME: *10-12 minutes*
COOKING TIME: *15 minutes*
SERVES: *4*

EACH SERVING: 194 Calories/ 35 Calories from Fat/ 17% Calories from Fat

Sichuan Noodles

This savory noodle dish is a specialty of Sichuan province. Ideal for lunch, brunch, or dinner, these noodles are a wonderful complement to any entree. To make a one-dish meal, simply add cooked chicken or turkey and some vegetables. Sichuan noodles are delicious hot or cold.

8 cups (2 quarts) cold water
¼ pound thin dry noodles or vermicelli

DRESSING
1 teaspoon sugar
¼ teaspoon black pepper
1 tablespoon Hunan chili paste
½ tablespoon oyster-flavored sauce
½ tablespoon sesame seed oil
½ tablespoon lite soy sauce
½ tablespoon wine vinegar
2 tablespoons diced scallions
1 teaspoon minced garlic

1. Bring 2 quarts of water to a rolling boil in a 4-quart saucepan. Add the noodles and cook, uncovered, for about 7 minutes – until they are tender to the bite.

2. While the noodles are cooking, combine the dressing ingredients and blend them well.

3. Drain and rinse the noodles in a colander with cold running water. Transfer them to a large bowl. Pour the dressing mixture over the noodles. Mix well and serve hot or cold.

PREPARATION TIME: *2 minutes*
COOKING TIME: *12-15 minutes*
YIELD: *3 cups cooked noodles*
SERVES: *6 (½ cup per serving)*

EACH SERVING: 91 Calories/ 13 Calories from Fat/ 14% Calories from Fat

week 2

Sweet & Sour Shrimp
Spinach & Mushrooms with Garlic
Sesame Noodles
387 Calories/ 100 Calories from Fat/ 26% Calories from Fat

Sweet & Sour Shrimp

A low-calorie – yet still tasty – version of a year-round favorite. The attractive play of colors and the rich blend of flavors in this dish will delight your diners.

1 pound large raw shrimp, about 20
1 large onion
½ large green or red bell pepper
1 8-ounce can pineapple chunks in unsweetened juice
1 tablespoon oil

MARINADE
2 teaspoons cornstarch
¼ teaspoon sugar
¼ teaspoon salt
¼ teaspoon black pepper
2 tablespoons dry white wine
½ tablespoon sesame seed oil

SEASONING
1 tablespoon sugar
1 teaspoon cornstarch
¼ teaspoon black pepper
¼ cup ketchup
2 tablespoons cider vinegar
2 tablespoons unsweetened pineapple juice
1 tablespoon lite soy sauce
1 tablespoon dry white wine

1. Shell the shrimp. With a sharp knife, make a ¼-inch cut in the back of each shrimp and devein it. Wash, drain and pat them dry with paper towels. Place them in medium-sized bowl.

2. Mix the marinade ingredients and add to the shrimp. Stir well and set aside for 30 minutes or longer.

3. Peel and halve the onion with the grain. Cut each half into thirds and then into 1-inch-long pieces and set aside. Wash and halve the green pepper. Cut the top off one half and clean out the seeds. Cut the pepper into 1-inch wide slices, then into 1-inch cubes. Set aside.

4. In a medium-sized bowl, mix the seasoning ingredients and set aside.

5. When the shrimp has marinated for at least 30 minutes, heat a wok on high for 30 seconds. Add the oil and swirl to coat the wok for 30 seconds longer. Add the onion and stir-toss for 1 minute. Add the pepper and stir-toss for 30 seconds. Add the seasoning mixture and bring to a quick boil. Add the shrimp with its marinade and stir-toss for another minute. Finally, add the pineapple chunks and mix well. Cook for 2 more minutes. Serve hot.

PREPARATION TIME:	*15 minutes*
MARINATING TIME:	*30 minutes or longer*
COOKING TIME:	*5-6 minutes*
SERVES:	*4*

EACH SERVING: 218 Calories/ 55 Calories from Fat/ 25% Calories from Fat

Spinach & Mushrooms with Garlic

Fresh spinach and mushrooms, stir-tossed gently with a hint of garlic, are a vegetable lover's delight. This dish nicely complements any meat, poultry or seafood entree.

1 pound fresh spinach
10 large mushrooms

1 teaspoon oil
1 tablespoon minced garlic

SEASONING
½ teaspoon salt
½ teaspoon sugar
½ teaspoon cornstarch
⅛ teaspoon black pepper
½ cup chicken broth
1 tablespoon dry white wine

1. Trim off the spinach roots and break the leaves in two. Wash them at least 3 times. Drain and pat dry.

2. Clean the mushrooms and thin-slice them about ¼-inch thick, cutting through both stems and caps.

3. In a medium bowl, mix the seasoning ingredients until smooth and set aside.

4. Heat a wok on high for 30 seconds. Add the oil and swirl to coat the wok evenly. Add garlic and stir-toss for 15 seconds. Add the seasoning mixture and bring it to a quick boil. Add the mushrooms and stir-toss for 1 minute. Add the spinach and stir-toss for another minute. Cover and cook on medium heat for 3 minutes.

5. Ladle to serving dish with a slotted spoon. Discard any excess sauce.

PREPARATION TIME:	*15-18 minutes*
COOKING TIME:	*8 minutes*
SERVES:	*4*

EACH SERVING: 57 Calories/ 16 Calories from Fat/ 28% Calories from Fat

Sesame Noodles

My low-calorie version of a traditional Beijing favorite. Roadside stands and fine restaurants alike boast of their special sesame noodles recipes. Try mine!

2 quarts cold water
¼ pound thin dry noodles or vermicelli
1 large scallion
1 small carrot
1 tablespoon water
1 tablespoon toasted sesame seeds

DRESSING
½ *teaspoon sugar*
¼ *teaspoon salt*
¼ *teaspoon black pepper*
1 tablespoon cider vinegar
1 tablespoon lite soy sauce
1 tablespoon sesame seed oil
1 teaspoon minced garlic

1. Bring 2 quarts of water to a rolling boil in a 4-quart saucepan . Add the vermicelli and cook, uncovered, for about 7 minutes – until they are tender to the bite.

2. While the noodles are cooking, fine-cut the carrot. Place the carrot slivers in a microwave-safe dish with 1 tablespoon of cold water and cook, covered, on high for 1 minute. Pour out the water and set the carrots aside. Fine-cut the scallion into slivers and set aside.

3. Drain the noodles in a colander under cold running water. Transfer them to a large bowl. Blend the dressing ingredients by shaking them in a small covered jar and pour this mixture over the noodles. Mix well, then add the toasted sesame seeds (see note below) and mix again. Garnish with the scallion and carrot slivers. Delicious hot or cold.

PREPARATION TIME:	*5-10 minutes*
COOKING TIME:	*12-15 minutes*
YIELD:	*3 cups cooked noodles*
SERVES:	*6 (½ cup per serving)*
NOTE:	*Sesame seeds need to be toasted to bring out their sweet, nutlike flavor. Spread the seeds on a cookie tray and bake them for 30 minutes in a 250-degree oven. Toasted seeds can be stored in an airtight covered jar for weeks – ready to use in other dishes.*
MAKE AHEAD:	*Yes, serve chilled.*

EACH SERVING: 112 Calories/ 29 Calories from Fat/ 26% Calories from Fat

week 3

Roasted Pork Chops
Asparagus with Lotus Root
Brown Rice
339 Calories/ 78 Calories from Fat/ 23% Calories from Fat

Roasted Pork Chops

My low-fat adaptation of the famed Cantonese roast pork, *char siu,* is every bit as tasty as the traditional dish. Longer marinating enhances the flavor of the pork. Overnight marinating is definitely preferable. Sliced cooked pork chops make a delicious topping on noodles and rice.

4 3-ounce pieces boneless pork chops, no more than ½-inch thick

MARINADE
¼ teaspoon 5-spice powder
¼ teaspoon black pepper
¼ teaspoon baking soda
2 tablespoons hoisin sauce
1 tablespoon chicken broth
2 tablespoons cold water
½ tablespoon lite soy sauce
1 tablespoon honey
1 tablespoon oyster-flavored sauce
1 tablespoon dry white wine
½ teaspoon minced garlic
1 tablespoon diced green scallions

1. Mix the marinade ingredients together until smooth in a large shallow dish with sides and set aside.

2. Wash the pork chops and pat them dry with paper towels. Trim the fat. Place the chops in the marinade dish and let them stand for 30 minutes or longer.

3. Preheat the oven to 425 degrees for 5 minutes. Place pork chops and marinade in a baking pan and roast for 10 minutes. Turn the chops over, baste them and roast for another 10 minutes.

4. Remove to a platter, top with the cooked marinade, and serve.

PREPARATION TIME:	*5 minutes*
MARINATING TIME:	*30 minutes or longer*
COOKING TIME:	*20 minutes*
SERVES:	*4*

EACH SERVING: 175 Calories/ 60 Calories from Fat/ 35% Calories from Fat

Asparagus with Lotus Root

I served this dish to some very special friends and they just loved it! You will too. Fresh lotus root is in a class all by itself – its exquisite natural design and crunchy texture is well worth a visit to the Chinese market.

1 pound fresh asparagus
½ pound length lotus root
½ teaspoon oil

SEASONING
1 teaspoon cornstarch
½ teaspoon sugar
dash black pepper
½ cup chicken broth
½ cup cold water
½ tablespoon oyster-flavored sauce
½ tablespoon dry white wine

1. Snap off and discard the tough end of each asparagus spear. (If you bend the stalk using both hands, they will usually break at the woody part of the stem.) Wash and drain the spears. Cut them into 2-inch lengths and set aside.

2. Cut off both ends of the lotus root and pare it. Slice it into ⅛-inch thick rounds. Set aside. Take time to notice the lovely design inside the root!

3. In a medium-sized bowl, mix the seasoning ingredients and set aside.

4. Heat a wok on high for 30 seconds. Add the oil and swirl to coat the work for 30 seconds longer. Add the lotus root and stir-toss for 15 seconds. Add the asparagus and stir-toss for 15 seconds longer. Add the seasoning, mix well, cover, and cook on high for about 4 minutes. Serve hot.

PREPARATION TIME: *8 to 10 minutes*
COOKING TIME: *5 ½ minutes*
SERVES: *6*

EACH SERVING: 48 Calories/ 13 Calories from Fat/ 24% Calories from Fat

Brown Rice

Brown rice has more bran and fiber and is also more nutritious than white rice. Its nutty taste and texture give it a distinctive appeal. The kernels need to be washed three times so they will absorb more water before cooking.

1 cup long grain brown rice
2 cups cold water

1. Place the rice in a 1-quart saucepan and rinse it three separate times with cold water. Pour off the excess water, cupping your hand over the rice grains. Do not use a colander. Add 2 cups of cold water to the rice and bring it to a boil, uncovered, over high heat.

2. When the water bubbles to the top of the saucepan, in about 10 minutes, turn the heat to medium and continue cooking uncovered. Stir the rice with chopsticks or a fork occasionally to prevent sticking.

3. After about 5 minutes when the water has almost evaporated, turn the heat to simmer. Cover the pot with a tight-fitting lid and steam for about 20 minutes. Do not lift the cover during this time.

4. When steaming is complete, fluff the rice with chopsticks. Let the rice stand, covered, until you are ready to serve.

PREPARATION TIME:	*2 minutes*
COOKING TIME:	*35 minutes*
YIELD:	*2½ cups of cooked rice*
SERVES:	*5 (½ cup per serving)*

EACH SERVING: 116 Calories/ 5 Calories from Fat/ 5% Calories from Fat

week 4

Tomato & Glassy Noodle Soup
Tofu Salad with Shrimp
White Rice
281 Calories/ 39 Calories from Fat/ 14% Calories from Fat

Tomato & Glassy Noodle Soup

An ideal soup to make when tomatoes are in season. Although inexpensive, this is an elegant soup.

4 cups chicken broth
1 2-ounce package glassy (cellophane) noodles
2 large well-ripened tomatoes
2 + 2 cups boiling water

2 egg whites, lightly beaten
2 tablespoons diced scallions

1. Bring the broth to a boil in a 2-quart covered saucepan, in about 7 minutes.

2. While the broth is cooking, place the glassy noodles in a medium-sized bowl and add 2 cups of boiling water. *Let them soak for 5 minutes only,* then drain and cut them into 2-inch lengths. Set aside.

3. In a medium-sized bowl, soak the tomatoes in 2 cups of boiling water for 1 minute. Skin, quarter, and cut them into small pieces. Set the tomatoes aside.

4. When the broth comes to a boil, add the tomatoes and noodles. Cover and cook the soup on medium heat, until it comes to a second boil, in about 3 minutes. Turn off the heat. Drizzle in the egg whites. Ladle to individual soup bowls, top with diced scallions, and serve. Diners add their own salt and pepper.

PREPARATION TIME:	*10-12 minutes*
COOKING TIME:	*10 minutes*
SERVES:	*6*
VARIATION:	*Use chicken broth for a totally vegetarian soup.*
MAKE AHEAD:	*Yes. Reserve adding the egg whites and scallions until you are ready to serve.*

EACH SERVING: 70 Calories/ 8 Calories from Fat/ 11 % Calories from Fat

Tofu Salad with Shrimp

Delicious as a one-dish meal – or as an entree with hot rice or noodles – this is a recipe you find yourself using in a number of ways. I like it as a filling for pita sandwiches!

1 cup cooked baby shrimp, frozen or fresh
2 cups boiling water
1 10½-ounce package Mori-Nu lite extra-firm tofu, drained
2 tablespoons diced scallions
1 teaspoon minced garlic

MARINADE
½ teaspoon sugar
½ teaspoon salt
⅛ teaspoon black pepper
1 teaspoon sesame seed oil
1 teaspoon wine vinegar
1 teaspoon Maggi seasoning

DRESSING
1 teaspoon sugar
⅛ teaspoon black pepper
1 tablespoon lite soy sauce
1 tablespoon oyster-flavored sauce
1 teaspoon sesame seed oil

1. Soak the shrimp in boiling water for 5 minutes. Drain and set aside.

2. Mix ingredients for the marinade in a medium bowl. Add the shrimp, mix well and let stand for 15 minutes or longer.

3. Drain the tofu, cut it into ½-inch cubes and drain again. Set aside.

4. Mix dressing ingredients in a large bowl. Add the tofu and toss well. Add the shrimp with its marinade and the diced scallions. Toss well and serve.

PREPARATION TIME:	*12-15 minutes*
MARINATING TIME:	*15 minutes*
SERVES:	*4*
NOTE:	*Mori-Nu lite tofu is truly low-fat – only 1% fat per serving. Other kinds of tofu have much high fat content. The extra-firm variety has more texture.*

EACH SERVING: 98 Calories/ 31 Calories from Fat/ 31% Calories from Fat

White Rice

It is very easy to make boiled rice the Chinese way, from scratch. Master this technique and you will always enjoy fluffy rice. If you eat rice often, an electric rice cooker is a good investment. You are guaranteed a perfect pot of rice every time.

1 cup long grain white rice
1¾ cups cold water

1. Put the rice in a 1-quart saucepan and rinse it twice with cold water. Pour off the excess water by cupping your hand over the rice grains. *Do not use a colander.* Add the cold water and bring the rice to a boil, uncovered, over high heat.

2. When the water bubbles to the top of the saucepan in about 7 minutes, turn the heat to medium and continue cooking uncovered. Stir with a fork or chopsticks occasionally to prevent sticking.

3. After about 5 minutes, when the water is almost evaporated, reduce the heat to simmer. Cover the saucepan with a tight-fitting lid and steam for about 20 minutes. Do not lift the lid during this time.

4. When the steaming is complete, fluff the rice with a fork or chopsticks. Replace the lid and let the rice stand until you are ready to serve.

PREPARATION TIME:	*2 minutes*
COOKING TIME:	*32 minutes*
YIELD:	*3½ cups cooked rice*
SERVES:	*7 (½ cup per serving)*
NOTE:	*Use the following formula to cook more rice: 2 cups of rice to 2¾ cups of water, yields 7 cups cooked rice; 3 cups of rice to 3¾ cups of water, yields about 10 cups of cooked rice. To succeed with these proportions, the rice must be rinsed twice (so that it can absorb some water) and drained by pouring the water off the rice instead of using a colander. Cup your hand over the rice as you pour off the water. Use larger saucepans for larger quantities and allow for longer cooking time.*

EACH SERVING: 113 Calories/ 0 Calories from Fat/ 0% Calories from Fat

week

1	Baked Turkey Cutlets Green Bean & Water Chestnut Salad Rice with Spinach & Carrots
2	Baked Prawns Stir-Tossed Cabbage with Ginger Fragrant Rice
3	Sesame Sirloin Meatballs Sweet Sugar Snap Peas Brown Rice
4	Baked Gourmet Beef Patties Asparagus Spears Cold-Tossed Noodles with Peanut Sauce

May
week 1

Baked Turkey Cutlets
Green Bean & Water Chestnut Salad
Rice with Spinach & Carrots
326 Calories/ 39 Calories from Fat/ 12% Calories from Fat

Baked Turkey Cutlets

This is one of my favorite marinades – ideal for roast pork as well as other meats or poultry. *Marinades are the key to Chinese cooking.* Try this tasty marinade on your turkey cutlets. You'll be delighted with the results. These cutlets are also great in sandwiches and, sliced into strips, as a topping for salads or noodles.

4 small (about 3 ounces each) turkey cutlets or fillets
½ teaspoon cornstarch
1 tablespoon cold water
¼ cup chicken broth

MARINADE
½ teaspoon 5-spice powder
dash of black pepper
2 tablespoons hoisin sauce
1 tablespoon oyster-flavored sauce
1 tablespoon honey
1 tablespoon whiskey or gin
1 teaspoon minced garlic
1 teaspoon grated onion
½ teaspoon grated gingerroot

1. Rinse the turkey cutlets and pat them dry with paper towels. Set aside.

2. Mix the cornstarch and cold water. In a large bowl, mix the marinade ingredients, add the cornstarch mix and blend until smooth. Add the turkey cutlets and let them stand for 30 minutes or longer. Turn them over several times to ensure even coating.

3. Preheat the oven to 400 degrees. Line a shallow baking pan with aluminum foil. After the cutlets have marinated for at least 30 minutes, place them side by side in the baking pan. Add ¼ cup chicken broth to the remaining marinade and spread over the cutlets.

4. Bake them for 5 minutes. Turn the cutlets, baste, and bake for another 5 minutes.

5. Remove them to a serving platter, top with the baking sauce and serve.

PREPARATION TIME: *8-10 minutes*
MARINATING TIME: *30 minutes*
COOKING TIME: *10 minutes*
SERVES: *4*
NOTE: *These cutlets are a healthy and delicious substitute for ham, beef or pork.*

EACH SERVING: 139 Calories/ 15 Calories from Fat/ 11% Calories from Fat

Green Bean & Water Chestnut Salad

What could be more appealing than this salad when green beans are in season? Coupled with thinly-sliced, crunchy water chestnuts, this dish is also a treat for the eyes.

1 pound fresh green beans
1 cup water
1 11-ounce can sliced water chestnuts
1 teaspoon minced garlic

DRESSING
1 teaspoon sugar
½ teaspoon salt
⅛ teaspoon black pepper
1 tablespoon water
1 tablespoon lite soy sauce
1 tablespoon oyster-flavored sauce
½ tablespoon sesame seed oil

1. Mix the dressing ingredients in a small bowl and set aside.

2. Wash the green beans and snip off the ends. Place them in a large microwave-safe bowl, add the water, cover and microwave on high for 9 minutes. Drain and refresh the beans with cold water to stop the cooking. Pat them dry.

3. Add the dressing and stir thoroughly to coat the beans. Add the sliced water chestnuts and minced garlic. Toss again to blend well and serve.

PREPARATION TIME: 8-10 minutes
COOKING TIME: 9 minutes
SERVES: 4
MAKE AHEAD: Yes, serve chilled.

EACH SERVING: 83 Calories/ 16 Calories from Fat/ 19% Calories from Fat

Rice with Spinach & Carrots

Once I tasted this dish at a fancy restaurant in San Antonio, I knew I had to include my version of it in my next collection. Steamed rice comes alive with chopped spinach and grated carrots.

½ cup rice
½ cup cold water
6 tablespoons chicken broth
2½ ounces chopped spinach, fresh or frozen (defrosted and drained)
½ small carrot, coarsely grated
salt to taste

SEASONING
¼ teaspoon sugar
a dash of black pepper
½ teaspoon sesame seed oil

1. Place the rice in a 2-quart saucepan and rinse it twice with cold water. To drain, pour off the excess water, cupping your hand over the grains. *Do not use a colander.* Add the fresh cold water, chicken broth, spinach and grated carrot. Bring the rice to a boil, uncovered, over high heat.

2. When the water bubbles to the top of the saucepan, in about 8 minutes, reduce the heat to simmer. Cover the pot with a tight-fitting lid and steam, without lifting the lid, for 20 minutes. Check to see if all the liquid has been absorbed. If not, continue steaming for a few minutes more.

3. When the rice is done, remove it from the heat, fluff it, replace the cover and let it stand until the other dishes are ready.

4. Just before serving, mix the seasoning and add it to the rice. Blend well and add salt if you wish. Serve immediately.

PREPARATION TIME: *5 minutes*
COOKING TIME: *33 minutes*
SERVES: *4 (½ cup servings)*
NOTE: *If you are using an automatic rice cooker, follow the same process. Add the spinach and carrot to the rice before steaming; add the seasoning when the rice is done and you are ready to serve it.*

EACH SERVING: 104 Calories/ 8 Calories from Fat/ 7% Calories from Fat

week 2

Baked Prawns
Stir-Tossed Cabbage with Ginger
Fragrant Rice
250 Calories/ 35 Calories from Fat/ 14% Calories from Fat

Baked Prawns

A truly gourmet way to prepare prawns or large shrimp – and you need only three ingredients! If you are using jumbo shrimp (about 12 to 15 to a pound), increase the broiling time by 2 to 3 minutes.

1 pound large shrimp, about 15-20 to the pound
15-20 six-inch-long bamboo skewers

MARINADE
1 teaspoon salt
1 tablespoon dry white wine
½ tablespoon whiskey

1. Cover the bamboo skewers with cold water and soak them for 10 minutes.

2. Holding each shrimp tightly, use kitchen shears to clip off the legs – but do not remove the shell. *Most large shrimp do not need to be deveined.* Rinse and pat them dry with paper towels. Set aside.

3. Combine the marinade ingredients in a small cup and spread on the shrimp. Use your fingers to spread the marinade and ensure that each shrimp is well-coated. Let them stand for 10 minutes or longer.

4. Set the oven rack about 4½ inches from the heat. Turn the oven to broil for 5 minutes. Line a baking pan with aluminum foil. Insert a skewer through each shrimp, *starting in the center* and continuing all the way to the tail. Place them side by side in the baking pan and broil for about 6 minutes – 2 or 3 minutes longer if using jumbo shrimp or prawns.

5. Serve immediately. Since the shrimp are still in the shell, they continue cooking as you remove them from the oven and take them to the table. By the time they reach the table, they are just right!

6. Serve with one or two dipping sauces. *See below for recipes.*

PREPARATION TIME:	*8-10 minutes*
SOAKING TIME:	*10 minutes*
MARINATING TIME:	*10 minutes*
COOKING TIME:	*6 - 8 minutes, depending on size*
SERVES:	*4*

EACH SERVING: 79 Calories/ 7 Calories from Fat/ 9% Calories from Fat

Quick Honey & Peanut Dipping Sauce
½ cup smooth peanut butter
¼ cup honey
¼ cup water

Combine the above ingredients in a blender and whip for 30 seconds. This dip can be made ahead and stored in the refrigerator for a least 2 weeks.

EACH SERVING: 64 Calories/ 37 Calories from Fat/ 54% Calories from Fat

Quick Sweet & Sour Dipping Sauce
½ cup peach preserves
½ cup marmalade preserves
½ cup wine vinegar
¼ teaspoon salt
⅛ teaspoon pepper

Follow the directions for Honey & Peanut Dipping Sauce.

EACH SERVING: 40 Calories/ 0 Calories from Fat/ 0% Calories from Fat

Hoisin Dipping Sauce

½ cup Hoisin sauce
¼ cup chicken broth
½ tablespoon wine vinegar
½ tablespoon sesame seed oil
⅛ teaspoon black pepper

Follow the directions for Honey & Peanut Dipping Sauce.

EACH SERVING: 19 Calories/ 8 Calories from Fat/ 40% Calories from Fat

Stir-Tossed Cabbage with Ginger

Delicious hot or cold, this dish lifts the lowly cabbage into elegance. Ginger root heightens the flavor and reduces the gaseous nature of the cabbage.

½ head medium-sized cabbage
1 small knob gingerroot
1 small onion
6 medium mushrooms
½ tablespoon oil
½ teaspoon salt

SEASONING
1 teaspoon sugar
½ teaspoon cornstarch
⅛ teaspoon black pepper
¼ cup chicken broth
2 tablespoons water
2 tablespoons lite soy sauce
1 tablespoon dry white wine

1. Mix the seasoning ingredients in a medium-sized bowl and set aside.

2. Rinse and core the cabbage. Cut 3-inch wedges and then slice each wedge crosswise into ¼-inch-wide strips. Set aside. Smash the gingerroot to release its flavor and set aside.

3. Peel and cut off the ends of the onion. Halve and thin-slice the onion with the grain. Set aside. Clean the mushrooms, thin-slice them through the cap and stem, and set them aside.

4. Heat a wok on high for 30 seconds. Add the oil and salt and swirl to coat the wok for 30 seconds longer. Add the gingerroot and stir-toss for 30 seconds. Add the onion slices and mushrooms. Stir-toss for 1 minute.

Add the cabbage and stir-toss for another minute. Add the seasoning mixture and stir-toss for 30 seconds. Cover the wok, lower the heat to medium-high and cook for 8 more minutes. Discard the gingerroot before serving.

PREPARATION TIME: *10-12 minutes*
COOKING TIME: *12 minutes*
SERVES: *4*

EACH SERVING: *72 Calories/ 20 Calories from Fat/ 27% Calories from Fat*

Fragrant Rice

Using jasmine rice instead of regular long grain rice introduces a fragrance the Chinese call *Hsiang mi,* "fragrant rice." Our recipe sweetens the pot even more by adding celery, scallions and cilantro and using chicken broth instead of water.

1 cup jasmine rice
1 teaspoon oil
3 stalks of celery, diced (preferably stalks near the heart)
1½ cups chicken broth
2 tablespoons diced scallions
2 tablespoons minced cilantro or Chinese parsley
½ teaspoon freshly ground white pepper

1. Put the rice in a large bowl and rinse it twice in cold water. Pour off the excess water by cupping your hand over the rice grains. Do not use a colander. Set aside.

2. Heat a 2-quart saucepan, add the oil and swirl it for 15 seconds to coat the pan. Add the celery and stir-toss for 45 seconds. Add the chicken broth and bring it to a boil. Add the rice and bring the pot to a second boil. Boil until the broth bubbles to the top, about 3 minutes. Turn the heat to medium and continue cooking, uncovered. Stir occasionally to prevent sticking.

3. When the broth is mostly evaporated (after about 5 minutes) reduce the heat to simmer, cover the pot with a tight-fitting lid and steam for 20 minutes more. Do not lift the lid during this time.

4. When the steaming is complete, fluff the rice, mix in the scallions, cilantro and pepper, fluff again, and serve immediately.

PREPARATION TIME: *5 minutes*
COOKING TIME: *31 minutes*
SERVES: *8 (½ cup servings)*

EACH SERVING: *99 Calories/ 8 Calories from Fat/ 9% Calories from Fat*

week 3

Sesame Sirloin Meatballs

A creative way to use sesame seeds and turn ground beef into a spectacular dish. These delicious treats may be served plain or with a dipping sauce like those used for Baked Prawns. *See Week 2 for May.*

¼ cup toasted sesame seeds
1 pound very lean ground sirloin
4 tablespoons diced scallions

SEASONING
2 tablespoons cornstarch
1 teaspoon sugar
½ teaspoon baking soda
½ teaspoon black pepper
2 tablespoons oyster-flavored sauce
1 tablespoon dry white wine

Spread toasted sesame seeds on a plate. Set aside.

1. In a large bowl, blend the seasoning ingredients until smooth. Add the ground beef, mix well and set aside. Let stand for 30 minutes or longer. Add the diced scallions and knead the mixture with your hands for 1 minute.

2. Scoop out about a teaspoon of meat and roll it into a 1-inch ball. Continue until you have used all the meat. You should have about 35 balls. Roll the meatballs in sesame seeds so they are well-coated. Set aside.

3. Line a cookie sheet with aluminum foil. Preheat the oven to 425 degrees. Bake the meatballs for 5 minutes. Turn and bake for another 5 minutes. Serve hot.

PREPARATION TIME:	*10 minutes*
MARINATING TIME:	*30 minutes*
COOKING TIME:	*10 minutes*

SERVES:	8
NOTES:	*This is a wonderful appetizer.*

To make toasted sesame seeds, place raw seeds on a cookie sheet and bake in a 250-degree oven for 30 minutes. Store leftover seeds in an airtight jar.

EACH SERVING: 117 Calories/ 43 Calories from Fat/ 38% Calories from Fat*
*These figures do not include the dipping sauces.

Sweet Sugar Snap Peas

Anytime you can find fresh sugar snap peas at your grocer's, snatch them up! When cooked this simple way, they delight any gourmand.

1 pound fresh sugar snap peas
2 50-cent-size slices gingerroot
½ tablespoon oil
½ teaspoon salt
½ cup chicken broth

1. With kitchen shears, snip the ends off the peapods. Rinse, drain and set aside.

2. Smash the gingerroot to release its full flavor. Set aside.

3. Heat a wok on high for 30 seconds. Add the oil and swirl to coat the wok for 30 seconds. Add the smashed gingerroot and stir-toss for 30 seconds. Add the salt and peapods. Stir-toss for 1 minute. Add the chicken broth, cover, and cook for 2½ minutes more.

4. Ladle to a bowl and serve.

PREPARATION TIME:	*6-8 minutes*
COOKING TIME:	*5 minutes*
SERVES:	*4*
MAKE AHEAD:	*Yes. Delicious hot or cold.*
NOTE:	*Fresh sugar snap peas have a firm, tender skin. No stringing necessary.*

EACH SERVING: 66 Calories/ 18 Calories from Fat/ 27% Calories from Fat

Brown Rice

Brown rice has more bran and fiber and is also more nutritious than white rice. Its nutty taste and texture give t a distinctive appeal. The kernels need to be washed three times so they will absorb more water before cooking.

1 cup long grain brown rice
2 cups cold water

1. Place the rice in a 1-quart saucepan and rinse it three separate times with cold water. Pour off the excess water, cupping your hand over the rice grains. Do not use a colander. Add 2 cups of cold water to the rice and bring it to a boil, uncovered, over high heat.

2. When the water bubbles to the top of the saucepan, in about 10 minutes, turn the heat to medium and continue cooking uncovered. Stir the rice with chopsticks or a fork occasionally to prevent sticking.

3. After about 5 minutes when the water has almost evaporated, turn the heat to simmer. Cover the pot with a tight-fitting lid and steam for about 20 minutes. Do not lift the cover during this time.

4. When steaming is complete, fluff the rice with chopsticks. Let the rice stand, covered, until you are ready to serve.

PREPARATION TIME:	*2 minutes*
COOKING TIME:	*35 minutes*
YIELD:	*2½ cups of cooked rice*
SERVES:	*5 (½ cup per serving)*

EACH SERVING: 116 Calories/ 5 Calories from Fat/ 5% Calories from Fat

week 4

Baked Gourmet Beef Patties
Asparagus Spears
Cold-Tossed Noodles with Peanut Sauce
289 Calories/ 74 Calories from Fat/ 26% Calories from Fat

Baked Gourmet Beef Patties

These meat patties are extraordinary – worthy of your most important guests. The seasoning and water chestnuts add a unique flavor and crunch. In addition to serving these patties with the noodles offered in this meal, try them on rice, pasta or hamburger buns.

1 pound very lean ground sirloin
12 canned water chestnuts, finely chopped

SEASONING
1 tablespoon cornstarch
1 teaspoon sugar
¼ teaspoon baking soda
¼ teaspoon black pepper
1 tablespoon lite soy sauce
1 tablespoon dry white wine
1 tablespoon oyster-flavored sauce
1 tablespoon cold water
1 teaspoon minced garlic
2 tablespoons diced scallions

1. In a large bowl, mix the marinade until smooth. Add the ground beef and mix well. Let stand for 30 minutes or longer. Add the chopped water chestnuts. Knead the beef mixture with your hands for 1 minute. Make 6 patties. Set aside.

2. Move the oven rack to about 4½ inches from the heat. Preheat the oven to 425 degrees. Line a cookie sheet with foil. Place the patties on the cookie sheet. For a medium-well-done patty, bake for 7 minutes, turn and bake for 7 more minutes. Increase or decrease the time by a couple of minutes on each side for well-done or rare patties.

3. Serve hot out of the oven.

PREPARATION TIME: *8-10 minutes*
MARINATING TIME: *30 minutes*
COOKING TIME: *14 minutes*
SERVES: *6*

EACH SERVING: 127 Calories/ 34 Calories from Fat/ 28% Calories from Fat

Asparagus Spears

A quick and simple way to serve asparagus at its best. Pick firm and unblemished spears. Take advantage of the lower prices when asparagus is in season and serve this dish often.

1½ pounds fresh asparagus spears
¼ cup chicken broth
2 teaspoons minced garlic

DRESSING
1 teaspoon sugar
¼ teaspoon black pepper
2 tablespoons lite soy sauce
½ teaspoon sesame seed oil

1. Snap off and discard the tough end of each asparagus spear. (If you bend the stalk using both hands, they will usually break at the woody part of the stem.) Wash and drain the spears. Place them in a microwave-safe dish. Add the chicken broth and garlic.

2. Cover the dish and microwave on high for 3 minutes. Pour off the liquid. Mix the dressing ingredients in a small cup and add to the cooked asparagus. Blend carefully but well.

3. This dish is delicious hot or cold. To chill for serving, refrigerate for at least ½ hour.

PREPARATION TIME:	*5 minutes*
COOKING TIME:	*3 minutes*
CHILLING TIME:	*30 minutes (optional)*
SERVES:	*4*
MAKE AHEAD:	*Yes, serve chilled.*

EACH SERVING: 46 Calories/ 13 Calories from Fat/ 26% Calories from Fat

Cold-Tossed Noodles with Peanut Sauce

A new way to enjoy peanut butter – as a dressing for noodles. A specilty of the Beijing region, this dish can be made ahead and chilled for later enjoyment.

¼ pound thin dry noodles or vermicelli
3 scallions with green tops
3 large cloves of garlic

DRESSING
½ teaspoon sugar
¼ teaspoon salt
⅛ teaspoon black pepper
2 tablespoons smooth peanut butter
2 tablespoons cold water
½ tablespoon lite soy sauce

1. Bring 2 quarts of water to a rolling boil in a 4-quart saucepan. Add the noodles and cook, uncovered, for about 7 minutes – until they are tender to the bite.

2. While the noodles are cooking, combine the dressing ingredients in a food processor and whip for 30 seconds. Set aside.

3. Wash and trim the scallions. Fine-dice the scallions including the green tops. Set aside. Mince the garlic and set aside.

4. When the noodles are cooked, rinse them in cold water and drain them well. Put them in a large serving bowl. Add the scallions, garlic and dressing. Toss well. Serve immediately or chilled.

PREPARATION TIME:	*10-12 minutes*
COOKING TIME:	*12-15 minutes*
YIELD:	*3 cups cooked noodles*
SERVES:	*6 (½ cup per serving)*
MAKE AHEAD:	*Yes, serve chilled.*
NOTE:	*It is important to use the food processor to get a well-blended dressing.*

EACH SERVING: 116 Calories/ 27 Calories from Fat/ 22% Calories from Fat

week

June

1	Chicken Fingers Sweet Sugar Snap Peas Rice with a Tropical Flair
2	Salmon Fillets with Hunan Chili Paste Spinach & Mushrooms with Garlic Sesame Noodles
3	Lettuce Wraps with Beef & Glassy Noodles Stir-Tossed Potato & Carrot Sticks Fragrant Rice
4	Steamed Turkey Meatballs Crunchy Peapods Noodles with Onion & Tomato Sauce

Chicken Fingers, Sweet Sugar Snap Peas
Rice with a Tropical Flair
330 Calories/ 67 Calories from Fat/ 20% Calories from Fat

Chicken Fingers

You can quickly prepare this all-time favorite right in your own kitchen – even when your pantry is skimpy. Chicken fingers make a great entree and a delicious appetizer.

1 8-ounce chicken breast
1 egg white
2 tablespoons toasted sesame seeds
vegetable oil spray

MARINADE
2 teaspoons cornstarch
½ teaspoon sugar
¼ teaspoon salt
¼ teaspoon baking soda
¼ teaspoon white pepper
1 tablespoon dry white wine
½ teaspoon oyster-flavored sauce

1. Mix the marinade ingredients in a medium-sized bowl and set aside.

2. Remove all skin and fat from the chicken breast. Cut it into strips, 2 inches long and ¼ inch wide, making about 26 strips. Place the strips in the marinade bowl. Marinate them for 30 minutes or longer.

3. Lightly spray the surface of a baking sheet with vegetable oil. Preheat the oven to 375 degrees.

4. Beat the egg white in a chilled metal bowl until frothy. Add the sesame seeds and set aside.

5. After the chicken has marinated for at least 30 minutes, add the egg white and sesame seed mixture. Stir well to coat the strips. Place the strips side by side on the baking sheet. Bake the strips for 5 minutes. Turn them over and continue baking for another 3 minutes.

6. Cool the Chicken Fingers for 5 minutes before removing them to a serving platter.

PREPARATION TIME:	*8-10 minutes*
MARINATING TIME:	*30 minutes*
COOKING TIME:	*8 minutes*
COOLING TIME:	*5 minutes*
SERVES:	*4*
NOTE:	*To make toasted sesame seeds, place raw seeds on a cookie sheet and bake in at 250-degrees for 30 minutes. Store leftover toasted seeds in an airtight jar.*

EACH SERVING: 100 Calories/ 24 Calories from Fat/ 24% Calories from Fat

Sweet Sugar Snap Peas

Anytime you can find fresh sugar snap peas at your grocer's, snatch them up! When cooked this simple way, they delight any gourmand.

1 pound fresh sugar snap peas
2 50-cent-size slices gingerroot
½ tablespoon oil
½ teaspoon salt
½ cup chicken broth

1. With kitchen shears, snip the ends off the peapods. Rinse, drain and set aside.

2. Smash the gingerroot to release its full flavor. Set aside.

3. Heat a wok on high for 30 seconds. Add the oil and swirl to coat the wok for 30 seconds. Add the smashed gingerroot and stir-toss for 30 seconds. Add the salt and peapods. Stir-toss for 1 minute. Add the chicken broth, cover, and cook for 2½ minutes more.

4. Ladle to a bowl and serve.

PREPARATION TIME:	*6-8 minutes*
COOKING TIME:	*5 minutes*
SERVES:	*4*
MAKE AHEAD:	*Yes. Delicious hot or cold.*

EACH SERVING: 66 Calories/ 18 Calories from Fat/ 27% Calories from Fat

Rice with a Tropical Flair

Bring Summer and sunshine into your meal with this tropical treat. Spiking the dish with vinegar gives it a sour bite that complements the sweet pineapple. I find this recipe a perfect way to use day-old rice. For a one-dish meal – simply add cooked chicken, steamed shrimp or leftover turkey.

2 cups day-old rice
4 egg whites, lightly beaten with 1 tablespoon Maggie seasoning
1 tablespoon oil
1 10-ounce can crushed pineapple in unsweetened juice, drained
1 tablespoon white vinegar
4 tablespoons diced scallions

Separate the rice clumps with your hands and set the rice aside.

1. Heat a wok on high for 1½ minutes. Add the oil and swirl to coat the work for 1½ minutes more until the wok is smoking. Pour in the egg white mixed with Maggie seasoning and stir quickly. Add the rice and stir-toss for 2 minutes. Add the pineapple. Stir-toss and mix for 1 minute. Add the vinegar and scallions and mix well with the rice. Turn the heat to medium, cover, and cook for 3 minutes.

2. Dish up the rice and serve hot.

PREPARATION TIME: *Less than 5 minutes*
COOKING TIME: *9 to 10 minutes*
SERVES: *5 (¾ cup per serving)*
EACH SERVING: 164 Calories/ 25 Calories from Fat/ 15% Calories from Fat

week 2

Salmon Fillets with Hunan Chili Paste
Spinach & Mushrooms with Garlic
Sesame Noodles
381 Calories/ 119 Calories from Fat/ 31% Calories from Fat

Salmon Fillets with Hunan Chili Paste

Rich and scrumptious, yet amazingly simple. A chef's recipe that you can serve with pride. Sichuan/Hunan food aficionados *love* this dish and will bribe you for the recipe.

4 4-ounce salmon fillets
2 quarts warm water
a 1-inch knob fresh gingerroot

SAUCE
1 teaspoon oil*
4 tablespoons diced scallions*
1 teaspoon grated gingerroot*
      * Keep the 3 items above separate from the following:
1 teaspoon sugar
1 teaspoon cornstarch
½ cup chicken broth
2 tablespoons Hunan chili paste
1 tablespoon oyster-flavored sauce
1 tablespoon whiskey

1. In a medium-sized bowl, mix the last 6 sauce ingredients until smooth. Set aside.

2. Rinse the salmon fillets and pat them dry with paper towels. Set them aside.

3. Put the warm water in a large saucepan with a lid. Smash the gingerroot knob flat to release its full flavor and add it to the saucepan. Cover and bring the water to a quick boil on high heat. Add the salmon. Cover and remove the saucepan from the heat to continue poaching the salmon.

4. The fillets should be done in about 3 minutes. Test to see if they have turned opaque and flake easily when touched with a fork. Carefully drain the fish fillets (they will be fragile) using a slotted spoon or spatula as you transfer them to a serving platter. Set aside.

5. To prepare the sauce, heat a wok on high for 30 seconds. Add the oil and swirl to evenly coat the wok for 30 seconds. Add the scallions and gingerroot and stir-toss for 30 seconds. Add the sauce mix and bring it to a quick boil. Mix well.

6. Ladle the sauce over the fillets. Serve immediately and get ready for the praise!

PREPARATION TIME:	*Less than 5 minutes*
COOKING TIME:	*5½ minutes*
SERVES:	*4*

EACH SERVING: 212 Calories/ 74 Calories from Fat/ 35% Calories from Fat

Spinach & Mushrooms with Garlic

Fresh spinach and mushrooms, stir-tossed gently with a hint of garlic, are a vegetable lover's delight. This dish nicely complements any meat, poultry or seafood entree.

1 pound fresh spinach
10 large mushrooms
1 teaspoon oil
1 tablespoon minced garlic

SEASONING
½ teaspoon salt
½ teaspoon sugar
½ teaspoon cornstarch
⅛ teaspoon black pepper
½ cup chicken broth
1 tablespoon dry white wine

1. Trim off the spinach roots and break the leaves in two. Wash them at least 3 times. Drain and pat dry.

2. Clean the mushrooms and thin-slice across each cap and stem. Set aside.

3. In a medium bowl, mix the seasoning ingredients until smooth and set aside.

4. Heat a wok on high for 30 seconds. Add the oil and swirl for 30 seconds to coat the wok. Add the garlic and stir-toss for 15 seconds. Add the seasoning mixture and bring it to a quick boil. Add the mushrooms and stir-toss for 1 minute. Add the spinach and stir-toss for another minute. Cover and cook on medium heat for 3 minutes.

5. Ladle to serving dish with a slotted spoon. Discard any excess sauce.

PREPARATION TIME: *15-18 minutes*
COOKING TIME: *8 minutes*
SERVES: *4*

EACH SERVING: 57 Calories/ 16 Calories from Fat/ 28% Calories from Fat

Sesame Noodles

My low-calorie version of a traditional Beijing favorite. Roadside stands and fine restaurants alike boast of their special sesame noodles recipes. Try mine!

2 quarts cold water
¼ pound thin dry noodles or vermicelli
1 large scallion
1 small carrot
1 tablespoon water
1 tablespoon toasted sesame seeds

DRESSING
½ teaspoon sugar
¼ teaspoon salt
¼ teaspoon black pepper
1 tablespoon cider vinegar
1 tablespoon lite soy sauce
1 tablespoon sesame seed oil
1 teaspoon minced garlic

1. Bring 2 quarts of water to a rolling boil in a 4-quart saucepan. Add the vermicelli and cook, uncovered, for about 7 minutes – until they are tender to the bite.

2. While the noodles are cooking, fine-cut the carrot. Place the carrot slivers in a microwave-safe dish with 1 tablespoon of cold water and cook, covered, on high for 1 minute. Pour out the water and set the carrots aside. Fine-cut the scallion into slivers and set aside.

3. Drain the noodles in a colander under cold running water. Transfer them to a large bowl. Blend the dressing ingredients by shaking them in a small covered jar and pour this mixture over the noodles. Mix well, then add the toasted sesame seeds (see note below) and mix again. Garnish with the scallion and carrot slivers. Delicious hot or cold.

PREPARATION TIME:	*5-10 minutes*
COOKING TIME:	*12-15 minutes*
YIELD:	*3 cups cooked noodles*
SERVES:	*6 (½ cup per serving)*
NOTE:	*Sesame seeds need to be toasted to bring out their sweet, nutlike flavor. Spread the seeds on a cookie sheet and bake them for 30 minutes in a 250-degree oven. Toasted seeds can be stored in an airtight covered jar for weeks – ready to use in other dishes.*
MAKE AHEAD:	*Yes, serve chilled.*

EACH SERVING: 112 Calories/ 29 Calories from Fat/ 26% Calories from Fat

week 3

Lettuce Wraps with Beef & Glassy Noodles
Stir-Tossed Potato & Carrot Sticks
Fragrant Rice
460 Calories/ 77 Calories from Fat/ 17% Calories from Fat

Lettuce Wraps with Beef & Glassy Noodles

A simple way to add pizazz to ground beef. Diners can have the fun of making their own lettuce wrap. There is no way to go wrong with this dish. It's easy, fun and delicious!

½ pound ground round steak
2 two-ounce packages of glassy noodles
4 cups boiling water
1 cup chicken broth
12 large lettuce leaves
6 cups cold water
ice cubes
½ tablespoon oil

MARINADE
1 teaspoon sugar
1 teaspoon cornstarch
⅛ teaspoon black pepper
1 tablespoon dry white wine
½ tablespoon oyster-flavored sauce
½ tablespoon lite soy sauce
2 tablespoons diced scallions

BINDER
¼ cup water
¼ cup chicken broth
½ teaspoon cornstarch

SPREAD
6 tablespoons of hoisin sauce

1. In a large bowl, blend the marinade ingredients until smooth. Add the ground beef. Stir well and let stand for 30 minutes or longer.

2. In a small bowl or jar, blend the ingredients for the binder and set aside.

3. Soak the glassy noodles in 4 cups of boiling water for 5 minutes. Drain, cut into 4-inch lengths. Set aside.

4. Remove the core from the head of lettuce. Discard any tough outer leaves. Carefully remove 12 large leaves. Place ice cubes and 6 cups of cold water in a large container and add the lettuce leaves to make them crisp. Drain them only minutes before serving.

5. Place the glassy noodles and 1 cup of chicken broth in a large microwave-safe dish. Cook on high for 3 minutes. Place in a serving bowl.

6. Heat a large wok on high for 30 seconds. Add the oil and swirl for 30 seconds to coat the wok. Stir the binder to be sure it is well-mixed and add it to the wok. Bring it to a boil. Quickly add the beef and marinade and cook on high for 3 minutes. Ladle to a serving dish.

7. Place the drained lettuce leaves on a serving platter.

8. Invite guests to wrap their own lettuce "rolls." First, they spread ½ tablespoon of hoisin sauce on a lettuce leaf, then add ¼ cup of glassy noodles and a heaping tablespoon of beef. Finally, they wrap the lettuce around the filling and enjoy a delicious sandwich. They'll keep coming back for more!

PREPARATION TIME: *12-15 minutes*
MARINATING TIME: *30 minutes*
COOKING TIME: *3½ minutes*
SERVES: *6 (2 lettuce wraps per diner)*

EACH SERVING: 167 Calories/ 34 Calories from Fat/ 20% Calories from Fat

Stir-Tossed Potato & Carrot Sticks

A colorful and tasty dish to cook when fresh leafy vegetables are not available. Potatoes and carrots, stir-tossed with a touch of garlic and oyster-flavored sauce, become irresistable. Fall back on this unique and easy dish when your pantry is running low.

3 medium potatoes
2 medium carrots
1 tablespoon oil
1 teaspoon minced garlic

SEASONING
1 teaspoon sugar
½ teaspoon salt
½ teaspoon cornstarch
2 cups chicken broth
2 tablespoons oyster-flavored sauce
1 tablespoon dry white wine
4 tablespoons diced scallions

1. Peel the potatoes and cut them into ½-inch slices. Stack 2 slices together and cut them into ¼-inch-wide strips no longer than 2 inches. Continue with the rest of the potato slices. Set them aside.

2. Peel the carrots and slice into strips about the same size as the potatoes. Set aside.

3. Mix the seasoning ingredients in a medium-sized bowl and set it aside.

4. Heat a wok on high for 30 seconds. Add the oil and swirl for 30 seconds to coat the wok. Add the garlic and stir-toss for 15 seconds. Add the seasoning mixture and bring it to a quick boil. Add the carrots and stir-toss for 1 minute. Add the potatoes, stir-toss, cover, and cook on medium heat for 10 minutes. Stir occasionally to prevent sticking.

5. Spoon to a dish and serve hot.

PREPARATION TIME: *10-12 minutes*
COOKING TIME: *15 minutes*
SERVES: *4*

EACH SERVING: 194 Calories/ 35 Calories from Fat/ 17% Calories from Fat

Fragrant Rice

Using jasmine rice instead of regular long grain rice introduces a fragrance the Chinese call *Hsiang mi*, "fragrant rice." Our recipe sweetens the pot even more by adding celery, scallions and cilantro and using chicken broth instead of water.

1 cup jasmine rice
1 teaspoon oil
3 stalks of celery, diced (preferably stalks near the heart)
1½ cups chicken broth
2 tablespoons diced scallions
2 tablespoons minced cilantro or Chinese parsley
½ teaspoon freshly ground white pepper

1. Put the rice in a large bowl and rinse it twice in cold water. Pour off the excess water by cupping your hand over the rice grains. Do not use a colander. Set aside.

2. Heat a 2-quart saucepan, add the oil and swirl it for 15 seconds to coat the pan. Add the celery and stir-toss for 45 seconds. Add the chicken broth and bring it to a boil. Add the rice and bring the pot to a second boil. Boil until the broth bubbles to the top, about 3 minutes. Turn the heat to medium and continue cooking, uncovered. Stir occasionally to prevent sticking.

3. When the broth is mostly evaporated (after about 5 minutes) reduce the heat to simmer, cover the pot with a tight-fitting lid and steam for 20 minutes more. Do not lift the lid during this time.

4. When the steaming is complete, fluff the rice, mix in the scallions, cilantro and pepper, fluff again, and serve immediately.

PREPARATION TIME: *5 minutes*
COOKING TIME: *31 minutes*
SERVES: *8 (½ cup servings)*

EACH SERVING: 99 Calories/ 8 Calories from Fat/ 9% Calories from Fat

week 4

Steamed Turkey Meatballs
Crunchy Peapods
Noodles with Onion & Tomato Sauce
377 Calories/ 66 Calories from Fat/ 18% Calories from Fat

Steamed Turkey Meatballs

This elegant yet simple dish is one of Donna's favorites. It serves well either as an entree or appetizer. The rice should be chilled so that it doesn't clump when you roll the turkey balls in it. Day-old rice is the easiest to work with.

12 whole canned water chestnuts
½ pound lean ground turkey
2 egg whites, lightly beaten
2½ cups cooked rice, chilled

SEASONING
½ teaspoon cornstarch
1 teaspoon sugar
½ teaspoon salt
a dash of black pepper
1 tablespoon lite soy sauce
1 tablespoon dry white wine
1 teaspoon oyster-flavored sauce
1 tablespoon minced garlic
1 tablespoon diced onion

1. Fill a Chinese steamer to the halfway mark with hot water from the tap. Cover the steamer and bring the water to a rolling boil in about 10 minutes.

2. Mix the seasoning ingredients in a small bowl and set aside. Quarter the water chestnuts. Place them with the ground turkey, egg white, and seasoning mixture in a food processor. Fine-chop for 1 minute.

3. Spread the cooked rice on a large plate. Scoop out 1 teaspoon of turkey mixture, shape it into a ball and place it on the rice. Continue until all the turkey mixture is used and you have about 40 turkey meatballs. Then roll each meatball, one at a time, in the cooked rice, coating it completely. Place the meatballs on plates that fit in your steamer.

4. Put the plates of meatballs on steamer racks. When the water in the steamer has come to a rolling boil, place the steamer racks in the steamer, cover, and steam on high for 7 minutes. Do not lift the lid during steaming.

5. Serve hot. Donna even likes them cold!

PREPARATION TIME:	*18-20 minutes*
COOKING TIME:	*7 minutes*
SERVES:	*6 as an entree; halve the recipe to serve it as an appetizer.*

EACH SERVING: 176 Calories/ 26 Calories from Fat/ 15% Calories from Fat

Crunchy Peapods

The delicate flavor and wonderful crunch of Chinese peapods are enhanced by this delicious dressing. Freshness is paramount: pick firm and unblemished pods and serve this recipe chilled.

pound fresh Chinese peapods
1 cup water

DRESSING
1½ teaspoons sugar
½ teaspoon salt
⅛ teaspoon black pepper
1 tablespoon lite soy sauce
½ tablespoon sesame seed oil
1 teaspoon minced garlic

1. Mix the dressing ingredients in a small bowl and set aside.

2. Wash and snip off the top of each peapod. Place the peapods in a large microwave-safe dish and add the cup of water. Cover and microwave on high for 2½ minutes. Drain the peapods and refresh them in cold water to stop the cooking. Pat them dry.

3. Pour the dressing over the peapods and toss to mix well. Serve immediately or chill and serve.

PREPARATION TIME: *8-10 minutes*
COOKING TIME: *2½ minutes*
CHILLING TIME: *30 minutes*
SERVES   *4*
MAKE AHEAD: *Yes*

EACH SERVING: 70 Calories/ 16 Calories from Fat/ 23% Calories from Fat

Noodles with Onion & Tomato Sauce

I love the look and taste of this simple noodle recipe. Only three ingredients! This dish can also serve as an entree – simply add cooked shrimp or cooked chunks of chicken, turkey or steak.

¼ pound thin dry noodles or vermicelli
8 cups cold water
1 large onion
2 cups boiling water
2 large tomatoes
1 tablespoon oil

SAUCE
½ tablespoon cornstarch
1 teaspoon sugar
¼ teaspoon black pepper

¼ *cup + 2 tablespoons ketchup*
2 tablespoons chicken broth
1 tablespoon dry white wine

1. Bring the water to a rolling boil in a 4-quart saucepan. Add the noodles and cook, uncovered, for about 7 minutes – until they are tender to the bite.

2. While the noodles are cooking, peel the onion and slice it with the grain into thin strips. Set aside.

3. In a medium-sized bowl, soak the tomatoes in 2 cups of boiling water for 1 minute. Drain them and use a paring knife to gently remove the skin. Quarter the peeled tomatoes and then crosscut each quarter into small pieces. Set aside in a small bowl.

4. Mix the sauce in a medium-sized bowl and set it aside.

5. When the noodles are done, rinse them in cold water, drain, and transfer them to a large serving bowl. Set aside.

6. Heat a wok on high for 30 seconds. Add the oil and swirl to coat the wok for 30 seconds. Add the onion and stir-toss for 1 minute. Add the tomatoes and stir-toss for another minute. Add the sauce and bring it to a boil. Cook 1 minute longer. Pour the sauce over the noodles and serve.

PREPARATION TIME:	*8 to 10 minutes*
COOKING TIME:	*18 minutes*
SERVES:	*6 (2/3 cup per serving)*
NOTE:	*When preparing this dish as an entree, double the recipe.*

EACH SERVING: 131 Calories/ 24 Calories from Fat/ 18% Calories from Fat

week

July

1	Lettuce Wraps with Chicken & Mushrooms Sweet Sugar Snap Peas Rice with a Tropical Flair
2	Baked Prawns Ivory & Jade Flowers Sichuan Noodles
3	Beef & Onions in Oyster Sauce Asparagus Spears Fragrant Rice
4	Shrimp Bisque Tofu Salad with Sesame Seeds, Peas & Capers Rice with Spinach & Carrots

Lettuce Wraps with Chicken & Mushrooms
Sweet Sugar Snap Peas
Rice with a Tropical Flair
335 Calories/ 71 Calories from Fat/ 21% Calories from Fat

Lettuce Wraps with Chicken & Mushrooms

Futuristic fooFun to prepare and eat. Full of flavor and fiber. Note that the recipe calls for *cooked* chicken. Add time for steaming a chicken breast, if you don't have cooked chicken on hand.

8 large lettuce leaves, preferably bib, but romaine or iceberg will do
2 quarts cold water with 1 cup ice cubes
1 cup cooked chicken
8 medium mushrooms
3 cups alfalfa sprouts
2 ounces fat-free mozzarella cheese, grated

DRESSING
½ teaspoon sugar
½ teaspoon salt
¼ teaspoon black pepper
¼ cup low-fat yogurt
½ tablespoon sesame seed oil
1 tablespoon lite soy sauce
1 teaspoon Dijon mustard

1. Soak the lettuce in the ice water for 15 minutes. Drain well and set aside.

2. While the lettuce is soaking, tear or cut the cooked chicken into thin slivers. Set aside in a medium-sized bowl.

3. Mix the dressing ingredients in a small covered jar and shake to blend. Pour the dressing over the chicken and mix well.

4. Clean and thin-slice the mushrooms through the cap and stem. Arrange the lettuce leaves, chicken, sliced mushrooms, alfalfa sprouts, and grated mozzarella cheese on a large platter or on separate plates.

5. Diners make their own "finger sandwich" by placing chicken, alfalfa sprouts, mushrooms, and grated mozzarella on a lettuce leaf and roll-wrapping it. They are scrumptious. Roll, wrap, and enjoy!

PREPARATION TIME: *12-15 minutes*
COOKING TIME: *20 minutes – if you don't already have cooked chicken, otherwise zero.*
SERVES: *4 as an entree, 8 as an appetizer*

EACH WRAP: 105 Calories/ 28 Calories from Fat/ 26% Calories from Fat

Sweet Sugar Snap Peas

Anytime you can find fresh sugar snap peas at your grocer's, snatch them up! When cooked this simple way, they delight any gourmand.

1 pound fresh sugar snap peas
2 50-cent-size slices gingerroot
½ tablespoon oil
½ teaspoon salt
½ cup chicken broth

1. With kitchen shears, snip the ends off the peapods. Rinse, drain and set aside.

2. Smash the gingerroot to release its full flavor. Set aside.

3. Heat a wok on high for 30 seconds. Add the oil and swirl to coat the wok for 30 seconds. Add the smashed gingerroot and stir-toss for 30 seconds. Add the salt and peapods. Stir-toss for 1 minute. Add the chicken broth, cover, and cook for 2½ minutes more.

4. Ladle to a bowl and serve.

PREPARATION TIME: *6-8 minutes*
COOKING TIME: *5 minutes*
SERVES: *4*

EACH SERVING: 66 Calories/ 18 Calories from Fat/ 27% Calories from Fat

Rice with a Tropical Flair

Bring Summer and sunshine into your meal with this tropical treat. Spiking the dish with vinegar gives it a sour bite that complements the sweet pineapple. I find this recipe a perfect way to use day-old rice. For a one-dish meal – simply add cooked chicken, steamed shrimp or leftover turkey.

2 cups day-old rice
4 egg whites, lightly beaten with 1 tablespoon Maggie seasoning
1 tablespoon oil
1 10-ounce can crushed pineapple in unsweetened juice, drained
1 tablespoon white vinegar
4 tablespoons diced scallions

1. Separate the rice clumps with your hands and set the rice aside.

2. Heat a wok on high for 1½ minutes. Add the oil and swirl to coat the work for 1½ minutes more until the wok is smoking. Pour in the egg white mixed with Maggie seasoning and stir quickly. Add the rice and stir-toss for 2 minutes. Add the pineapple. Stir-toss and mix for 1 minute. Add the vinegar and scallions and mix well with the rice. Turn the heat to medium, cover, and cook for 3 minutes.

3. Dish up the rice and serve hot.

PREPARATION TIME: *Less than 5 minutes*
COOKING TIME: *9 to 10 minutes*
SERVES: *5 (¾ cup per serving)*

EACH SERVING: 164 Calories/ 25 Calories from Fat/ 15% Calories from Fat

week 2

Baked Prawns
Ivory & Jade Flowers
Sichuan Noodles
244 Calories/ 40 Calories from Fat/ 16% Calories from Fat

Baked Prawns

A truly gourmet way to prepare prawns or large shrimp – and you need only three ingredients! If you are using jumbo shrimp (about 12 to 15 to a pound), increase the broiling time by 2 to 3 minutes.

1 pound large shrimp, about 15-20 to the pound
15-20 six-inch-long bamboo skewers

MARINADE
1 teaspoon salt
1 tablespoon dry white wine
½ tablespoon whiskey

1. Cover the bamboo skewers with cold water and soak them for 10 minutes.

2. Holding each shrimp tightly, use kitchen shears to clip off the legs – but do not remove the shell. *Most large shrimp do not need to be deveined.* Rinse and pat them dry with paper towels. Set aside.

3. Combine the marinade ingredients in a small cup and spread on the shrimp. Use your fingers to spread the marinade and ensure that each shrimp is well-coated. Let them stand for 10 minutes or longer.

4. Set the oven rack about 4½ inches from the heat. Turn the oven to broil for 5 minutes. Line a baking pan with aluminum foil. Insert a skewer through each shrimp, *starting in the center* and continuing all the way to the tail. Place them side by side in the baking pan and broil for about 6 minutes – 2 or 3 minutes longer if using jumbo shrimp or prawns.

5. Serve immediately. Since the shrimp are still in the shell, they continue cooking as you remove them from the oven and take them to the table. By the time they reach the table, they are just right!

6. Serve with one or two dipping sauces. *See below for recipes.*

PREPARATION TIME:	*8-10 minutes*
SOAKING TIME:	*10 minutes*
MARINATING TIME:	*10 minutes*
COOKING TIME:	*6 - 8 minutes, depending on size*
SERVES:	*4*

EACH SERVING: 79 Calories/ 7 Calories from Fat/ 9% Calories from Fat

Quick Honey & Peanut Dipping Sauce
½ cup smooth peanut butter
¼ cup honey
¼ cup water

Combine the above ingredients in a blender and whip for 30 seconds. This dip can be made ahead and stored in the refrigerator for a least 2 weeks.

EACH SERVING: 64 Calories/ 37 Calories from Fat/ 54% Calories from Fat

Quick Sweet & Sour Dipping Sauce

½ cup peach preserves
½ cup marmalade preserves
½ cup wine vinegar
¼ teaspoon salt
⅛ teaspoon pepper

Follow the directions for Honey & Peanut Dipping Sauce.

EACH SERVING: 40 Calories/ 0 Calories from Fat/ 0% Calories from Fat

Hoisin Dipping Sauce

½ cup Hoisin sauce
¼ cup chicken broth
½ tablespoon wine vinegar
½ tablesppon sesame seed oil
⅛ teaspoon black pepper

Follow the directions for Honey & Peanut Dipping Sauce.

EACH SERVING: 19 Calories/ 8 Calories from Fat/ 40% Calories from Fat

Ivory & Jade Flowers

Stir-tossed and flavored with garlic and oyster sauce, these vegetables are simply scrumptious. This is one of Donna's favorite recipes. Try to stop at just one helping.

½ large head cauliflower
1 stalk broccoli
½ tablespoon oil
1 teaspoon minced garlic
½ teaspoon salt

SEASONING
1 teaspoon sugar
½ teaspoon cornstarch

¼ teaspoon black pepper
2 tablespoons chicken broth
2 tablespoons water
1 tablespoon oyster-flavored sauce
1 tablespoon dry white wine

1. Rinse the cauliflower. Remove and discard the leaves and cut off about 1 inch of the stem. Separate flowerets and cut them into 2-inch long pieces. Half or quarter the thicker pieces.

2. Rinse the broccoli and cut the flowerets into 2-inch lengths. Peel the broccoli stalk with a paring knife. Slice the stalk into ½-inch diagonal slices or roll-cut it into 2-inch lengths. Set aside.

3. Mix the seasoning ingredients in a medium-sized bowl and set aside.

4. Heat a wok on high for 30 seconds. Add the oil and swirl to coat the wok for 30 seconds longer. Add the garlic and salt. Stir-toss for 15 seconds. Add the cauliflower. Stir-toss for 1 minute. Add the broccoli and stir-toss for 1 more minute. Pour in the seasoning mixture, blend well, cover, and cook for 3 minutes longer. This dish may be served hot or cold.

PREPARATION TIME:	*8-10 minutes*
COOKING TIME:	*7 minutes*
SERVES:	*4*

EACH SERVING: 74 Calories/ 20 Calories from Fat/ 25% Calories from Fat

Sichuan Noodles

This savory noodle dish is a specialty of Sichuan province. Ideal for lunch, brunch, or dinner, these noodles are a wonderful complement to any entree. To make a one-dish meal, simply add cooked chicken or turkey and some vegetables. Sichuan noodles are delicious hot or cold.

8 cups (2 quarts) cold water
¼ pound thin dry noodles or vermicelli

DRESSING
1 teaspoon sugar
¼ teaspoon black pepper
1 tablespoon Hunan chili paste
½ tablespoon oyster-flavored sauce
½ tablespoon sesame seed oil

½ tablespoon lite soy sauce
½ tablespoon wine vinegar
2 tablespoons diced scallions
1 teaspoon minced garlic

1. Bring 2 quarts of water to a rolling boil in a 4-quart saucepan. Add the noodles and cook, uncovered, for about 7 minutes – until they are tender to the bite.

2. While the noodles are cooking, combine the dressing ingredients and blend them well.

3. Drain and rinse the noodles in a colander with cold running water. Transfer them to a large bowl. Pour the dressing mixture over the noodles. Mix well and serve hot or cold.

PREPARATION TIME:	*2 minutes*
COOKING TIME:	*12-15 minutes*
YIELD:	*3 cups cooked noodles*
SERVES:	*6 (½ cup per serving)*

EACH SERVING: 91 Calories/ 13 Calories from Fat/ 14% Calories from Fat

week 3

Beef & Onions in Oyster Sauce
Asparagus Spears
Fragrant Rice
301 Calories/ 80 Calories from Fat/ 27% Calories from Fat

Beef & Onions in Oyster Sauce

Robust and satisfying! The oyster-flavored sauce gives this beef dish a distinctive and full-flavored taste. Your dinner guests will beg for the recipe.

8 ounces round steak, partially frozen, trimmed
1 large onion
4 large fresh mushrooms
1 tablespoon oil

MARINADE
1 teaspoon sugar
1 teaspoon cornstarch
½ teaspoon baking soda
¼ teaspoon black pepper
1 tablespoon oyster-flavored sauce
2 tablespoons dry white wine

SAUCE
½ teaspoon cornstarch
¼ teaspoon sugar
¼ teaspoon black pepper
6 tablespoons chicken broth
½ tablespoon oyster-flavored sauce
½ tablespoon lite soy sauce
1 tablespoon dry white wine

1. Cut the round steak lengthwise into slices, 1½ x ⅛ inches. Place the steak in medium-sized bowl and set aside.

2. Blend the marinade ingredients in a small bowl until smooth and add to the beef. Toss to coat the meat well and let it stand for 30 minutes or longer.

3. Mix the ingredients for the sauce in a medium-sized bowl and set aside.

4. Cut off the ends of the onion, peel and halve it along the grain. Cut each half into ¼-inch wide slices. Set aside. Clean and thin-slice the mushrooms through the caps and stems into ¼-inch slices. Set aside.

5. When the beef has marinated for at least 30 minutes, heat a large wok on high for 30 seconds. Add the oil and swirl to coat the wok for 30 seconds. Add the onion and stir-toss for 1 minute. Add the mushrooms and cook for 30 seconds longer. Stir the sauce to be sure it is well-mixed, add it to the wok and bring the dish to a quick boil. Add the beef and marinade. Stir-toss for 3 more minutes. Ladle to a serving bowl and serve with the other hot dishes.

PREPARATION TIME:	15 minutes
MARINATING TIME:	30 minutes or longer
COOKING TIME:	6 minutes
SERVES:	4

EACH SERVING: 156 Calories/ 59 Calories from Fat/ 38% Calories from Fat

Asparagus Spears

A quick and simple way to serve asparagus at its best. Pick firm and unblemished spears. Take advantage of the lower prices when asparagus is in season and serve this dish often.

1½ pounds fresh asparagus spears
¼ cup chicken broth
2 teaspoons minced garlic

DRESSING
1 teaspoon sugar
¼ teaspoon black pepper
2 tablespoons lite soy sauce
½ teaspoon sesame seed oil

1. Snap off and discard the tough end of each asparagus spear. (If you bend the stalk using both hands, they will usually break at the woody part of the stem.) Wash and drain the spears. Place them in a microwave-safe dish. Add the chicken broth and garlic.

2. Cover the dish and microwave on high for 3 minutes. Pour off the liquid. Mix the dressing ingredients in a small cup and add to the cooked asparagus. Blend carefully but well.

3. This dish is delicious hot or cold. To chill for serving, refrigerate for at least ½ hour.

PREPARATION TIME:	*5 minutes*
COOKING TIME:	*3 minutes*
CHILLING TIME:	*30 minutes (optional)*
SERVES:	*4*
MAKE AHEAD:	*Yes, serve chilled.*

EACH SERVING: 46 Calories/ 13 Calories from Fat/ 26% Calories from Fat

Fragrant Rice

Using jasmine rice instead of regular long grain rice introduces a fragrance the Chinese call *Hsiang mi,* "fragrant rice." Our recipe sweetens the pot even more by adding celery, scallions and cilantro and using chicken broth instead of water.

1 cup jasmine rice
1 teaspoon oil

3 stalks of celery, diced (preferably stalks near the heart)
1½ cups chicken broth
2 tablespoons diced scallions
2 tablespoons minced cilantro or Chinese parsley
½ teaspoon freshly ground white pepper

1. Put the rice in a large bowl and rinse it twice in cold water. Pour off the excess water by cupping your hand over the rice grains. Do not use a colander. Set aside.

2. Heat a 2-quart saucepan, add the oil and swirl it for 15 seconds to coat the pan. Add the celery and stir-toss for 45 seconds. Add the chicken broth and bring it to a boil. Add the rice and bring the pot to a second boil. Boil until the broth bubbles to the top, about 3 minutes. Turn the heat to medium and continue cooking, uncovered. Stir occasionally to prevent sticking.

3. When the broth is mostly evaporated (after about 5 minutes) reduce the heat to simmer, cover the pot with a tight-fitting lid and steam for 20 minutes more. Do not lift the lid during this time.

4. When the steaming is complete, fluff the rice, mix in the scallions, cilantro and pepper, fluff again, and serve immediately.

PREPARATION TIME: *5 minutes*
COOKING TIME: *31 minutes*
SERVES: *8 (½ cup servings)*

EACH SERVING: 99 Calories/ 8 Calories from Fat/ 9% Calories from Fat

week 4

Shrimp Bisque
Tofu Salad with Sesame Seeds, Peas & Capers
Rice with Spinach & Carrots
354 Calories/ 61 Calories from Fat/ 17% Calories from Fat

Shrimp Bisque

This is my tasty low-fat version of a classical favorite. Whenever I am in need of cheer, this soup is sure to lift my spirits – and make my guests feel very special.

6 large fresh shrimp, shelled
2 egg whites, lightly beaten
3 cups clam juice, bottled or canned
1 cup 2% milk

MARINADE
1 teaspoon cornstarch
½ teaspoon sugar
⅛ teaspoon salt
a dash of black pepper
1 tablespoon cold water
½ tablespoon whiskey
1 teaspoon sesame seed oil

BINDER
1 tablespoon cornstarch
2 tablespoons cold water

GARNISH
2 tablespoons cilantro leaves

1. Wash and drain the shrimp. Pat them dry with paper towels. Cut them shrimp in half, lengthwise, then cut each half into pea-sized pieces.

2. Mix the marinade in a medium-sized bowl and add the shrimp. Let stand for 15 minutes or longer.

3. Combine the stock and milk in a 2-quart saucepan and bring to a boil, in about 5 minutes. Mix the binder and *slowly* add it to the soup. When the soup comes to a second boil, add the shrimp and cook for 1 minute.

4. Turn off the heat and slowly drizzle in the egg whites. Stir with a pair of chopsticks or fork to make wispy strings of the egg white. Ladle to individual soup bowls, garnish with cilantro leaves, and serve.

PREPARATION TIME:	*5-8 minutes*
MARINATING TIME:	*5 minutes*
COOKING TIME:	*7 minutes*
SERVES:	*4*
NOTE:	*While whiskey adds a special zest, dry white wine tastes good too.*

EACH SERVING: 137 Calories/ 26 Calories from Fat/ 19% Calories from Fat

Tofu Salad with Sesame Seeds, Peas & Capers

As you acquire a taste for tofu, you will discover its chameleon charm – it quickly"takes on the colors" of any seasoning. Here the blended flavors of capers and sesame seeds give the tofu a distinctively delicate flavor.

1 10½-ounce package Mori-Nu extra-firm lite tofu, drained
4 cups hot water
1½ cups frozen peas, thawed
1 tablespoon toasted sesame seeds

DRESSING
2 teaspoon sugar
½ teaspoon salt
¼ teaspoon white pepper
1½ tablespoons lite soy sauce
1 teaspoon sesame seed oil
1 tablespoon bottled capers, drained
1½ teaspoon minced garlic

GARNISH
2 tablespoons diced scallions

1. Cut the tofu into ½-inch cubes and place in a large bowl. Place the peas in a seperate large bowl. Add 2 cups of hot water to each bowl and let stand for 10 minutes. Layer a colander with paper towels and, using a slotted spoon add the tofu. Drain it for 5 minutes. Return the tofu to the large bowl and set aside. Drain the peas and add them to the tofu. Set aside.

2. Place the dressing ingredients in a blender and fine-chop for 30 seconds. Pour it over the tofu and toss to blend well. Add the sesame seeds and toss again.

3. Garnish with the diced scallions and serve.

PREPARATION TIME: *10-12 minutes*
SOAKING TIME: *10 minutes*
SERVES: *4*
NOTE: *Mori-Nu lite tofu is truly low-fat – only 1% fat per serving. Other kinds of tofu have much high fat content. The extra-firm variety has more texture.*

Toast sesame seeds to bring out their sweet, nutlike flavor. Spread the seeds on a cookie sheet and bake them for 30 minutes in the oven at 250 degrees.

EACH SERVING: 113 Calories/ 27 Calories from Fat/ 24% Calories from Fat

Rice with Spinach & Carrots

Once I tasted this dish at a fancy restaurant in San Antonio, I knew I had to include my version of it in my next collection. Steamed rice comes alive with chopped spinach and grated carrots.

½ cup rice
½ cup cold water
6 tablespoons chicken broth
2½ ounces chopped spinach, fresh or frozen (defrosted and drained)
½ small carrot, coarsely grated
salt to taste

SEASONING
¼ teaspoon sugar
dash of black pepper
½ teaspoon sesame seed oil

1. Place the rice in a 2-quart saucepan and rinse it twice with cold water. To drain, pour off the excess water, cupping your hand over the grains. *Do not use a colander.* Add the fresh cold water, chicken broth, spinach and grated carrot. Bring the rice to a boil, uncovered, over high heat.

2. When the water bubbles to the top of the saucepan, in about 8 minutes, reduce the heat to simmer. Cover the pot with a tight-fitting lid and steam, without lifting the lid, for 20 minutes. Check to see if all the liquid has been absorbed. If not, continue steaming for a few minutes more.

3. When the rice is done, remove it from the heat, fluff it, replace the cover and let it stand until the other dishes are ready.

4. Just before serving, mix the seasoning and add it to the rice. Blend well and add salt if you wish. Serve immediately.

PREPARATION TIME:	*5 minutes*
COOKING TIME:	*33 minutes*
SERVES:	*4 (½ cup servings)*
NOTE:	*If you are using an automatic rice cooker, follow the same process. Add the spinach and carrot to the rice before steaming; add the seasoning when the rice is done and you are ready to serve it.*

EACH SERVING: 104 Calories/ 8 Calories from Fat/ 7% Calories from Fat

week August

1	Baked Turkey Cutlets Chinese Broccoli & Straw Mushrooms Cold-Tossed Noodles with Peanut Sauce
2	Sweet & Sour Shrimp Shanghai String Bean Salad White Rice
3	Meatballs in Hot & Spicy Sauce Chinese Tossed Salad Sesame Noodles
4	Sichuan Chicken Crunchy Peapods Rice with Crabmeat & Mushrooms

August week 1

Baked Turkey Cutlets
Chinese Broccoli & Straw Mushrooms
Cold-Tossed Noodles with Peanut Sauce
335 Calories/ 55 Calories from Fat/ 16% Calories from Fat

Baked Turkey Cutlets

This is one of my favorite marinades – ideal for roast pork as well as other meats or poultry. *Marinades are the key to Chinese cooking.* Try this tasty marinade on your turkey cutlets. You'll be delighted with the results. These cutlets are also great in sandwiches and, sliced into strips, as a topping for salads or noodles.

4 small (about 3 ounces each) turkey cutlets or fillets
½ teaspoon cornstarch
1 tablespoon cold water
¼ cup chicken broth

MARINADE
½ teaspoon 5-spice powder
dash of black pepper
2 tablespoons hoisin sauce
1 tablespoon oyster-flavored sauce
1 tablespoon honey
1 tablespoon whiskey or gin
1 teaspoon minced garlic
1 teaspoon grated onion
½ teaspoon grated gingerroot

1. Rinse the turkey cutlets and pat them dry with paper towels. Set aside.

2. Mix the cornstarch and cold water. In a large bowl, mix the marinade ingredients, add the cornstarch mix and blend until smooth. Add the turkey cutlets and let them stand for 30 minutes or longer. Turn them over several times to ensure even coating.

3. Preheat the oven to 400 degrees. Line a shallow baking pan with aluminum foil. After the cutlets have marinated for at least 30 minutes, place them side by side in the baking pan. Add ¼ cup chicken broth to the remaining marinade and spread over the cutlets.

4. Bake them for 5 minutes. Turn the cutlets, baste, and bake for another 5 minutes.

5. Remove them to a serving platter, top with the baking sauce and serve.

PREPARATION TIME:	*8-10 minutes*
MARINATING TIME:	*30 minutes*
COOKING TIME:	*10 minutes*
SERVES:	*4*
NOTE:	*These cutlets are a healthy and delicious substitute for ham, beef or pork.*

EACH SERVING: 139 Calories/ 15 Calories from Fat/ 11% Calories from Fat

Chinese Broccoli & Straw Mushrooms

The Chinese love their greens – especially Chinese broccoli or *gai lan*. *Gai lan* is prized for its taste and crunchy texture. This classic dish, served at the best Chinese restaurants and roadside stands, is one of my favorites. Use the stalks (they are tender and tasty) as well as the leaves.

1½ pounds fresh Chinese broccoli
2 quarts of warm water
a 1-inch knob of gingerroot, smashed
2 tablespoons dry white wine
1 teaspoon sugar
1 8-ounce can tiny peeled straw mushrooms, drained

SAUCE
½ teaspoon sugar
½ teaspoon cornstarch
¼ cup chicken broth
2 tablespoons water from the mushrooms

2 tablespoons oyster-flavored sauce
½ tablespoon sesame seed oil

1. Bring the warm water, wine, sugar and gingerroot to a quick boil in a 6-quart covered saucepan.

2. Rinse and drain the *gai lan* without cutting or breaking the stalks and leaves. Set aside.

3. When the water comes to a boil, add the *gai lan* and cook, uncovered, for 4 to 5 minutes – until it turns bright, vibrant green. Drain and arrange artistically on a large platter.

4. While the *gai lan* is cooking, mix the sauce ingredients in a large bowl, and add the straw mushrooms. Microwave on high for 2 minutes and then pour over the *gai lan*.

5. Delicious hot or cold.

PREPARATION TIME:	*Less than 5 minutes*
COOKING TIME:	*12 minutes*
MAKE AHEAD:	*Yes, serve cold.*
SERVES:	*6*

EACH SERVING: 80 Calories/ 13 Calories from Fat/ 16% Calories from Fat

Cold-Tossed Noodles with Peanut Sauce

A new way to enjoy peanut butter – as a dressing for noodles. A specialty of the Beijing region, this dish can be made ahead and chilled for later enjoyment.

¼ pound thin dry noodles or vermicelli
3 scallions with green tops
3 large cloves of garlic

DRESSING
½ teaspoon sugar
¼ teaspoon salt
⅛ teaspoon black pepper
2 tablespoons smooth peanut butter
2 tablespoons cold water
½ tablespoon lite soy sauce

1. Bring 2 quarts of water to a rolling boil in a 4-quart saucepan. Add the noodles and cook, uncovered, for about 7 minutes – until they are tender to the bite.

2. While the noodles are cooking, combine the dressing ingredients in a food processor and whip for 30 seconds. Set aside.

3. Wash and trim the scallions. Fine-dice the scallions including the green tops. Set aside. Mince the garlic and set aside.

4. When the noodles are cooked, rinse them in cold water and drain them well. Put them in a large serving bowl. Add the scallions, garlic and dressing. Toss well. Serve immediately or chilled.

PREPARATION TIME:	*10-12 minutes*
COOKING TIME:	*12-15 minutes*
YIELD:	*3 cups cooked noodles*
SERVES:	*6 (½ cup per serving)*
MAKE AHEAD:	*Yes, serve chilled.*
NOTE:	*It is important to use the food processor to get a well-blended dressing.*

EACH SERVING: 116 Calories/ 27 Calories from Fat/ 22% Calories from Fat

week 2

Sweet & Sour Shrimp
Shanghai String Bean Salad
White Rice
395 Calories/ 72 Calories from Fat/ 18% Calories from Fat

Sweet & Sour Shrimp

A low-calorie – yet still tasty – version of a year-round favorite. The attractive play of colors and the rich blend of flavors in this dish will delight your diners.

1 pound large raw shrimp, about 20
1 large onion
½ large green or red bell pepper
1 8-ounce can pineapple chunks in unsweetened juice
1 tablespoon oil

MARINADE
2 teaspoons cornstarch
¼ teaspoon sugar
¼ teaspoon salt
¼ teaspoon black pepper
2 tablespoons dry white wine
½ tablespoon sesame seed oil

SEASONING
1 tablespoon sugar
1 teaspoon cornstarch
¼ teaspoon black pepper
¼ cup ketchup
2 tablespoons cider vinegar
2 tablespoons unsweetened pineapple juice
1 tablespoon lite soy sauce
1 tablespoon dry white wine

1. Shell the shrimp. With a sharp knife, make a ¼-inch cut in the back of each shrimp and devein it. Wash, drain and pat them dry with paper towels. Place them in medium-sized bowl.

2. Mix the marinade ingredients and add to the shrimp. Stir well and set aside for 30 minutes or longer.

3. Peel and halve the onion with the grain. Cut each half into thirds and then into 1-inch-long pieces and set aside. Wash and halve the green pepper. Cut the top off one half and clean out the seeds. Cut the pepper into 1-inch wide slices, then into 1-inch cubes. Set aside.

4. In a medium-sized bowl, mix the seasoning ingredients and set aside.

5. When the shrimp has marinated for at least 30 minutes, heat a wok on high for 30 seconds. Add the oil and swirl to coat the wok for 30 seconds longer. Add the onion and stir-toss for 1 minute. Add the pepper and stir-toss for 30 seconds. Add the seasoning mixture and bring to a quick boil. Add the shrimp with its marinade and stir-toss for another minute. Finally, add the pineapple chunks and mix well. Cook for 2 more minutes. Serve hot.

PREPARATION TIME:	*15 minutes*
MARINATING TIME:	*30 minutes or longer*
COOKING TIME:	*5-6 minutes*
SERVES:	*4*

EACH SERVING: 218 Calories/ 55 Calories from Fat/ 25% Calories from Fat

Shanghai String Bean Salad

A fail-proof recipe for fresh green beans. For maximum flavor, prepare this dish the day before.

1 pound fresh green beans
2 quarts cold water

DRESSING
½ teaspoon sugar
⅛ teaspoon black pepper
2 tablespoons wine vinegar
2 tablespoons Maggi seasoning
½ tablespoon sesame seed oil
1 teaspoon minced garlic

1.   Place the cold water in a large saucepan with a lid and bring to a boil, in about 5 minutes. While the water is boiling, snip off the ends of the beans with a pair of kitchen shears. Wash, drain and set them aside.

2.   Mix the dressing ingredients in a large bowl and set aside.

3.   When the water is boiling, add the beans, cover and cook on high for 5 minutes. Drain and refresh them in cold water to stop the cooking. Add the beans to the bowl with the dressing. Toss to coat them well. Refrigerate, covered, for an hour or overnight. Tossing the beans from time to time helps the dressing seep into the beans.

PREPARATION TIME: *6-8 minutes*
COOKING TIME: *10 minutes*
REFRIGERATION: *1 hour or overnight*
SERVES: *4*

EACH SERVING: 64 Calories/ 17 Calories from Fat/ 25% Calories from Fat

White Rice

It is very easy to make boiled rice the Chinese way, from scratch. Master this technique and you will always enjoy fluffy rice. If you eat rice often, an electric rice cooker is a good investment. You are guaranteed a perfect pot of rice every time.

1 cup long grain white rice
1¾ cups cold water

1.   Put the rice in a 1-quart saucepan and rinse it twice with cold water. Pour off the excess water by cupping

your hand over the rice grains. *Do not use a colander.* Add the cold water and bring the rice to a boil, uncovered, over high heat.

2. When the water bubbles to the top of the saucepan in about 7 minutes, turn the heat to medium and continue cooking uncovered. Stir with a fork or chopsticks occasionally to prevent sticking.

3. After about 5 minutes, when the water is almost evaporated, reduce the heat to simmer. Cover the saucepan with a tight-fitting lid and steam for about 20 minutes. Do not lift the lid during this time.

4. When the steaming is complete, fluff the rice with a fork or chopsticks. Replace the lid and let the rice stand until you are ready to serve.

PREPARATION TIME:	*2 minutes*
COOKING TIME:	*32 minutes*
YIELD:	*3½ cups cooked rice*
SERVES:	*7 (½ cup per serving)*
NOTE:	*Use the following formula to cook more rice: 2 cups of rice to 2¾ cups of water, yields 7 cups cooked rice; 3 cups of rice to 3¾ cups of water, yields about 10 cups of cooked rice. To succeed with these proportions, the rice must be rinsed twice (so that it can absorb some water) and drained by pouring the water off the rice instead of using a colander. Cup your hand over the rice as you pour off the water.*

EACH SERVING: 113 Calories/ 0 Calories from Fat/ 0% Calories from Fat

week 3

Meatballs in Hot & Spicy Sauce
Chinese Tossed Salad
Sesame Noodles
303 Calories/ 74 Calories from Fat/ 24% Calories from Fat

Meatballs in Hot & Spicy Sauce

An easy-to-make dish for those who have a taste for the hot and spicy. This versatile recipe serves well as an appetizer or an entree.

1 pound very lean ground sirloin

SEASONING
1½ tablespoons cornstarch
1 teaspoon sugar
¼ teaspoon baking soda
¼ teaspoon black pepper
½ tablespoon lite soy sauce
1 tablespoon dry white wine
½ tablespoon oyster-flavored sauce
1 tablespoon cold water
1 small onion, finely minced

HOT & SPICY SAUCE
½ tablespoon cornstarch
1½ teaspoons sugar
1 cup cold water
2 tablespoons Hunan chili paste
2 tablespoons oyster-flavored sauce
2 tablespoons ketchup

1. In a large bowl, blend the seasoning ingredients until smooth. Add the ground beef and mix well. Let stand for 30 minutes or longer. Knead the mixture for 1 minute. Roll the meat into 1-inch balls. Repeat until you use all the meat. You should have 35 to 40 meatballs. Set aside. Wetting your hands from time to time will help you make smoother meatballs.

2. Mix ingredients for the hot and spicy sauce in a medium bowl and set aside.

3. Heat a wok on high for 30 seconds. Add the hot and spicy sauce and bring it to a boil. Turn the heat to medium and add the meatballs. Cover and cook for 3 minutes. Roll the meatballs over gently with a spatula and cook for another 3 minutes. Remove the meatballs and sauce to a serving dish. Serve piping hot.

PREPARATION TIME:	*25-30 minutes*
MARINATING TIME:	*30 minutes*
COOKING TIME:	*8 minutes*
SERVES:	*5*
NOTE:	*Adjust the amount of Hunan chili paste to suit your taste. Different brands also vary in intensity. Experiment for best results.*

EACH SERVING: 167 Calories/ 43 Calories from Fat/ 26 % Calories from Fat

Chinese Tossed Salad

Combine your favorite lettuce (iceberg, romaine, bib, Boston) with bok choy and Napa cabbage, add straw mushrooms for elegance and pizazz and enjoy tossed green salad Chinese style.

¾ pound lettuce
¼ pound bok choy
¼ pound Napa cabbage
½ sweet red pepper
1 8-ounce can tiny peeled straw mushrooms, drained

1. Chill individual salad plates.

2. Rinse the greens and break them into bite-sized pieces or cut them on the bias into strips. Toss and mix the greens in a large bowl and then dish them out onto the chilled plates.

3. Trim the pepper and thin slice it into strips. Add several strips to each plate for color and flavor.

4. Top each serving with a tablespoon scoop of straw mushrooms and serve with a side bowl of Quick Sweet and Sour Dressing.

PREPARATION TIME:	*6 to 8 minutes*
COOKING TIME:	*None*
SERVES:	*8*
NOTE:	*The tiny peeled straw mushrooms are the most attractive. Ask your Chinese grocer for that special variety.*

EACH SERVING: 24 Calories/ 2 Calories from Fat/ 7% Calories from Fat

Quick Sweet & Sour Dressing

½ cup peach preserves
½ cup marmalade preserves
½ cup wine vinegar
¼ teaspoon salt
⅛ teaspoon pepper

Combine the above ingredients in a blender and whip for 30 seconds. This dressing can be made ahead and stored in the refrigerator for a least 2 weeks.

EACH SERVING: 40 Calories/ 0 Calories from Fat/ 0% Calories from Fat

Sesame Noodles

My low-calorie version of a traditional Beijing favorite. Roadside stands and fine restaurants alike boast of their special sesame noodles recipes. Try mine!

2 quarts cold water
¼ pound thin dry noodles or vermicelli
1 large scallion
1 small carrot
1 tablespoon water
1 tablespoon toasted sesame seeds

DRESSING
½ teaspoon sugar
¼ teaspoon salt
¼ teaspoon black pepper
1 tablespoon cider vinegar
1 tablespoon lite soy sauce
1 tablespoon sesame seed oil
1 teaspoon minced garlic

1. Bring 2 quarts of water to a rolling boil in a 4-quart saucepan. Add the vermicelli and cook, uncovered, for about 7 minutes – until they are tender to the bite.

2. While the noodles are cooking, fine-cut the carrot. Place the carrot slivers in a microwave-safe dish with 1 tablespoon of cold water and cook, covered, on high for 1 minute. Pour out the water and set the carrots aside. Fine-cut the scallion into slivers and set aside.

3. Drain the noodles in a colander under cold running water. Transfer them to a large bowl. Blend the dressing ingredients by shaking them in a small covered jar and pour this mixture over the noodles. Mix well, then add the toasted sesame seeds (see note below) and mix again. Garnish with the scallion and carrot slivers. Delicious hot or cold.

PREPARATION TIME:	*5-10 minutes*
COOKING TIME:	*12-15 minutes*
YIELD:	*3 cups cooked noodles*
SERVES:	*6 (½ cup per serving)*
NOTE:	*Toast sesame seeds to bring out their sweet, nutlike flavor. Spread the seeds on a cookie sheet and bake them for 30 minutes in a 250-degree oven. Toasted seeds can be stored in an airtight container for weeks .*

MAKE AHEAD: *Yes, serve chilled.*

EACH SERVING: 112 Calories/ 29 Calories from Fat/ 26% Calories from Fat

week 4

Sichuan Chicken
Crunchy Peapods
Rice with Crabmeat & Mushrooms
413 Calories/ 73 Calories from Fat/ 18% Calories from Fat

Sichuan Chicken

Delicious baked or grilled, this spicy, plan-ahead dish is well worth the 2-hour marinating time.

4 *4-ounce chicken thighs, skinned and boned*
      OR
2 *8-ounce chicken breasts, skinned and boned*

MARINADE
2 teaspoons sugar
1 teaspoon cornstarch
¼ teaspoon baking soda
¼ teaspoon black pepper
1½ cups cold water
2 tablespoons dry white wine
1½ tablespoons Hunan chili paste
1½ tablespoons oyster-flavored sauce
2 tablespoons scallions, diced
1 teaspoon garlic, minced
½ teaspoon gingerroot, grated

1. Wash the chicken, remove all fat, pat dry with paper towels. Set aside.

2. In a large bowl, mix the marinade and add the chicken. Refrigerate for two hours or more. Turn the meat occasionally to assure that the seasoning penetrates all the flesh.

3. When the chicken is almost through marinating, preheat the oven to 375 degrees. Line a baking pan with

foil and put the chicken and its marinade in it. Bake for 25 minutes; turn it over and continue baking for another 20 minutes. Baste the chicken as you turn it.

4. Remove the chicken to a serving platter and top with any sauce left in the baking pan. Serve hot.

PREPARATION TIME:	*12 minutes*
MARINATING TIME:	*2 hours*
COOKING TIME:	*45 minutes*
SERVES:	*4*
NOTE:	*Use more or less Hunan chili paste to make the dish more or less spicy: fiery hot is 2 to 3 tablespoons; medium hot, 1 to 1½; and mild, ½ to ¾. Different brands also vary in intensity. Experiment for best results – and remember, it is much easier to add more chili paste than it is to cook more noodles, so begin with a mild mix!*

*EACH SERVING WITH **WHITE** MEAT:*
159 Calories/ 14 Calories from Fat/9% Calories from Fat

*EACH SERVING WITH **DARK** MEAT:*
139 Calories/ 31 Calories from Fat/ 23% Calories from Fat

Crunchy Peapods

The delicate flavor and wonderful crunch of Chinese peapods are enhanced by this delicious dressing. Freshness is paramount: pick firm and unblemished pods and serve this recipe chilled.

1 pound fresh Chinese peapods
1 cup water

DRESSING
1½ teaspoons sugar
½ teaspoon salt
⅛ teaspoon black pepper
1 tablespoon lite soy sauce
½ tablespoon sesame seed oil
1 teaspoon minced garlic

1. Mix the dressing ingredients in a small bowl and set aside.

2. Wash and snip off the top of each peapod. Place the peapods in a large microwave-safe dish and add the

cup of water. Cover and microwave on high for 2½ minutes. Drain the peapods and refresh them in cold water to stop the cooking. Pat them dry.

3. Pour the dressing over the peapods and toss to mix well. Serve immediately or chill and serve.

PREPARATION TIME: *8-10 minutes*
COOKING TIME: *2½ minutes*
CHILLING TIME: *30 minutes*
SERVES   *4*
MAKE AHEAD: *Yes*

EACH SERVING: 70 Calories/ 16 Calories from Fat/ 23% Calories from Fat

Rice with Crabmeat & Mushrooms

This dish is a great crowd-pleaser and my 7-year-old grandson's favorite. In fact, I created it especially for him. Around out house it's called "Ian's Rice Recipe"! *Note that this recipe presumes you have already cooked a pot of white rice and have it ready!*

6 ounces of crab meat
6 medium mushrooms
1 small onion
4 medium-sized fresh asparagus spears

SEASONING
¼ tablespoon cornstarch
½ tablespoon cold water
¼ teaspoon salt
dash of white pepper
½ tablespoon Maggi seasoning
½ tablespoon dry white wine
6 tablespoons chicken broth
6 tablespoons 2% milk
½ tablespoon oil
2 cups freshly-cooked hot rice

1. Cut the crab into 1-inch pieces. Set aside.

2. Clean the mushrooms and trim the stems to ½ inch from the cap. Thin-slice through cap and stem and set aside.

3. Trim and peel the onion. Halve and thin-slice it with the grain. Set aside.

4. Snap off and discard the tough end of each asparagus spear. (If you bend the stalk using both hands, it will usually break at the woody part of the stem.) Wash, drain, and thin-slice the spears diagonally into ½-inch pieces. Set aside.

5. In a large bowl, mix the cornstarch with cold water, blending until smooth. Add the other ingredients for the seasoning, mix well and set aside.

6. Heat a wok on high for 30 seconds. Add the oil and swirl to coat the sides of the wok for 30 seconds. Add the onion and stir-toss for 30 seconds. Add the mushrooms and stir-toss for 30 seconds. Add the asparagus and stir-toss for 30 seconds. Add the seasoning mixture and bring to a boil. Add the crab meat, cover and cook for 2 minutes.

7. Dish up the hot rice, top it with the crab and vegetable mixture and serve immediately.

PREPARATION TIME:	*10-12 minutes*
COOKING TIME:	*5½ minutes*
SERVES:	*4*
NOTE:	*Imitation crab can be used in this recipe.*

EACH SERVING: 204 Calories/ 26 Calories from Fat/ 13% Calories from Fat

week September

1	Chicken with Anise & Peppercorns Peapod, Egg, Tomato & Mushroom Salad Brown Rice
2	Salmon Fillets with Hunan Chili Paste Sweet Sugar Snap Peas Sichuan Noodles
3	Pork Chops Baked in Hoisin Sauce Crunchy Peapods White Rice
4	Turkey Vegetable Soup Curried Shrimp on Bean Sprouts Rice with a Tropical Flair

Sep tem ber week 1

Chicken with Anise & Peppercorns
Peapod, Egg, Tomato & Mushroom Salad
Brown Rice
391 Calories/ 70 Calories from Fat/ 18% Calories from Fat

Chicken with Anise & Peppercorns

A gentle way to cook chicken that will delight your diners. Use this recipe to prepare cooked chicken to use in many other dishes: appetizers, soups, salads and sandwiches.

4 chicken thighs, about 1½ pounds

MARINADE
1 teaspoon sugar
½ teaspoon salt
½ teaspoon black pepper
2 tablespoon dry white wine
1 tablespoon white vinegar
½ tablespoon anise pieces or 4 dried star anise, broken into small pieces
½ tablespoon dry peppercorns

1. Wash the chicken thighs and pat them dry with paper towels. Leave the skin on the thighs to retain the moisture, but trim off the fat and any excess skin. Place the thighs in a shallow dish that fits into your steamer and set aside. Mix the marinade ingredients in a small bowl and spread evenly over the chicken. Let it stand for at least 2 hours. Overnight marinating is even better.

2. Fill a Chinese steamer to the halfway mark with hot tap water. Cover the steamer and bring the water to a rolling boil in about 10 minutes. Place the dish of chicken on the steamer rack, and put the rack in the steamer. Cover and steam on high for 40 minutes. Do not lift the lid during steaming.

3. Let the chicken cool for 10 minutes before serving.

PREPARATION TIME: *12-15 minutes*
MARINATING TIME: *A minimum of 2 hours, overnight marinating is better.*
COOKING TIME: *50 minutes*
COOLING TIME: *10 minutes*

EACH SERVING: 176 Calories/ 47 Calories from Fat/ 28% Calories from Fat

Peapod, Egg, Tomato & Mushroom Salad

An unusual combination, but unrivaled in taste, color and presentation. A winner every time!

8 medium dried black Chinese mushrooms
1 cup warm water
12 ounces fresh Chinese peapods
1 cup cold water
4 small firm tomatoes
4 hard-boiled eggs, whites only

MARINADE
½ teaspoon sugar
⅛ teaspoon black pepper
¼ cup cold water
1 tablespoon oyster-flavored sauce
½ tablespoon dry white wine
½ tablespoon sesame seed oil

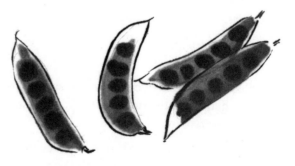

1. Mix the marinade ingredients in a small bowl and set aside. Chill the salad plates in the refrigerator.

2. Place the dried black Chinese mushrooms, caps down, in a microwave-safe bowl with 1 cup of warm water. Cover and microwave on high for 5 minutes. Drain the mushrooms, refresh them in cold water and squeeze them dry. Remove and discard the stems. Thin-slice the caps. Return them to the microwave bowl. Add the marinade mixture, blend well, cover, and microwave on high for 4 minutes. Mix well and set aside.

3. Wash and drain the peapods. Snip off the tops. Place the peapods in a large microwave-safe dish and add

1 cup of cold water. Cover and microwave on high for 3 minutes. Drain the peapods and refresh them with cold water to stop the cooking. Drain them again and pat them dry. Divide the peapods into 4 equal portions.

4. Halve the tomatoes and cut each half into 3 wedges. Set aside. Quarter the hard-boiled eggs and discard the yolks. Halve each quarter and set aside.

5. Arrange the peapods like a sunburst on individual pre-chilled salad plates. Add the tomato wedges and egg in alternate patterns. Place ¼ portion of the Chinese mushrooms and marinade in the center of each plate.

6. Serve as is or add a salad dressing of your choice.

PREPARATION TIME: *12-15 minutes*
COOKING TIME: *12 minutes*
SERVES: *4*
MAKE AHEAD: *Yes*

EACH SERVING: 99 Calories/ 18 Calories from Fat/ 18% Calories from Fat

Brown Rice

Brown rice has more bran and fiber and is also more nutritious than white rice. Its nutty taste and texture give it a distinctive appeal. The kernels need to be washed three times so they will absorb more water before cooking.

1 cup long grain brown rice
2 cups cold water

1. Place the rice in a 1-quart saucepan and rinse it three separate times with cold water. Pour off the excess water, cupping your hand over the rice grains. Do not use a colander. Add 2 cups of cold water to the rice and bring it to a boil, uncovered, over high heat.

2. When the water bubbles to the top of the saucepan, in about 10 minutes, turn the heat to medium and continue cooking uncovered. Stir the rice with chopsticks or a fork occasionally to prevent sticking.

3. After about 5 minutes when the water has almost evaporated, turn the heat to simmer. Cover the pot with a tight-fitting lid and steam for about 20 minutes. Do not lift the cover during this time.

4. When steaming is complete, fluff the rice with chopsticks. Let the rice stand, covered, until you are ready to serve.

PREPARATION TIME: *2 minutes*
COOKING TIME: *35 minutes*
YIELD: *2½ cups of cooked rice*

SERVES: *5 (½ cup per serving)*

EACH SERVING: 116 Calories/ 5 Calories from Fat/ 5% Calories from Fat

Salmon Fillets with Hunan Chili Paste
Sweet Sugar Snap Peas
Sichuan Noodles
369 Calories/ 105 Calories from Fat/ 28% Calories from Fat

Salmon Fillets with Hunan Chili Paste

Rich and scrumptious, yet amazingly simple. A chef's recipe that you can serve with pride. Sichuan/Hunan food aficionados *love* this dish and will bribe you for the recipe.

4 4-ounce salmon fillets
2 quarts warm water
a 1-inch knob fresh gingerroot

SAUCE
1 teaspoon oil*
4 tablespoons diced scallions*
1 teaspoon grated gingerroot*
        * Keep the 3 items above separate from the following:
1 teaspoon sugar
1 teaspoon cornstarch
½ cup chicken broth
2 tablespoons Hunan chili paste
1 tablespoon oyster-flavored sauce
1 tablespoon whiskey

1. In a medium-sized bowl, mix the last 6 sauce ingredients until smooth. Set aside.

2. Rinse the salmon fillets and pat them dry with paper towels. Set them aside.

3. Put the warm water in a large saucepan with a lid. Smash the gingerroot knob flat to release its full flavor and add it to the saucepan. Cover and bring the water to a quick boil on high heat. Add the salmon. Cover and remove the saucepan from the heat to continue poaching the salmon.

4. The fillets should be done in about 3 minutes. Test to see if they have turned opaque and flake easily when touched with a fork. Carefully drain the fish fillets (they will be fragile) using a slotted spoon or spatula as you transfer them to a serving platter. Set aside.

5. To prepare the sauce, heat a wok on high for 30 seconds. Add the oil and swirl to evenly coat the wok for 30 seconds. Add the scallions and gingerroot and stir-toss for 30 seconds. Add the sauce mix and bring it to a quick boil. Mix well.

6. Ladle the sauce over the salmon fillets. Serve immediately and get ready for the praise!

PREPARATION TIME: *Less than 5 minutes*
COOKING TIME: *5½ minutes*
SERVES: *4*

EACH SERVING: 212 Calories/ 74 Calories from Fat/ 35% Calories from Fat

Sweet Sugar Snap Peas

Anytime you can find fresh sugar snap peas at your grocer's, snatch them up! When cooked this simple way, they delight any gourmand.

1 pound fresh sugar snap peas
2 50-cent-size slices gingerroot
½ tablespoon oil
½ teaspoon salt
½ cup chicken broth

1. With kitchen shears, snip the ends off the peapods. Rinse, drain and set aside.

2. Smash the gingerroot to release its full flavor. Set aside.

3. Heat a wok on high for 30 seconds. Add the oil and swirl to coat the wok for 30 seconds. Add the smashed gingerroot and stir-toss for 30 seconds. Add the salt and peapods. Stir-toss for 1 minute. Add the chicken broth, cover, and cook for 2½ minutes more.

4. Ladle to a bowl and serve.

PREPARATION TIME: *6-8 minutes*

COOKING TIME: 5 minutes
SERVES: 4
MAKE AHEAD: Yes. Delicious hot or cold.
NOTE: Fresh sugar snap peas have a firm, tender skin. No stringing necessary.

EACH SERVING: 66 Calories/ 18 Calories from Fat/ 27% Calories from Fat

Sichuan Noodles

This savory noodle dish is a specialty of Sichuan province. Ideal for lunch, brunch, or dinner, these noodles are a wonderful complement to any entree. To make a one-dish meal, simply add cooked chicken or turkey and some vegetables. Sichuan noodles are delicious hot or cold.

8 cups (2 quarts) cold water
¼ pound thin dry noodles or vermicelli

DRESSING
1 teaspoon sugar
¼ teaspoon black pepper
1 tablespoon Hunan chili paste
½ tablespoon oyster-flavored sauce
½ tablespoon sesame seed oil
½ tablespoon lite soy sauce
½ tablespoon wine vinegar
2 tablespoons diced scallions
1 teaspoon minced garlic

1. Bring 2 quarts of water to a rolling boil in a 4-quart saucepan. Add the noodles and cook, uncovered, for about 7 minutes – until they are tender to the bite.

2. While the noodles are cooking, combine the dressing ingredients and blend them well.

3. Drain and rinse the noodles in a colander with cold running water. Transfer them to a large bowl. Pour the dressing mixture over the noodles. Mix well and serve hot or cold.

PREPARATION TIME: 2 minutes
COOKING TIME: 12-15 minutes
YIELD: 3 cups cooked noodles
SERVES: 6 (½ cup per serving)

EACH SERVING: 91 Calories/ 13 Calories from Fat/ 14% Calories from Fat

week 3

Pork Chops Baked in Hoisin Sauce

A dish that is both rich and elegant. Hoisin sauce and 5-spice powder marry well and together add zest and fragrance to the chops.

4 boneless center cut pork chops, very lean
2 large scallions, diced
1 cup chicken broth

MARINADE
1 teaspoon cornstarch
½ teaspoon 5-spice powder
¼ teaspoon baking soda
¼ teaspoon black pepper
3 tablespoons hoisin sauce
2 tablespoons cold water
1 tablespoon whiskey
1 tablespoon honey
½ tablespoon oyster-flavored sauce
½ teaspoon minced garlic

1. Trim all fat from the pork chops. Rinse and pat them dry with paper towels. Place the chops in a baking dish with sides and enough space so they do not overlap.

2. Mix the marinade and add it to the chops. Marinate for 30 minutes or longer. Turning the chops occasionally will ensure that both sides are well coated with the marinade.

3. Preheat the oven to 375 degrees.

4. Just before baking, add the diced scallions and chicken broth to the chops, mixing them in with the marinade. Bake the chops on a mid-oven rack for 10 minutes. Turn, baste, and bake them for another 10 minutes.

5. Ladle the chops and sauce onto a platter. Serve right away.

PREPARATION TIME:	12-15 minutes
MARINATING TIME:	30 minutes
COOKING TIME:	20 minutes
SERVES:	4
NOTE:	Dry white wine may be substituted for the whiskey, but the dish is not as tasty. Try marinating the chops overnight for an even tastier flavor.

EACH SERVING: 195 Calories/ 58 Calories from Fat/ 30% Calories from Fat

Crunchy Peapods

The delicate flavor and wonderful crunch of Chinese peapods are enhanced by this delicious dressing. Freshness is paramount: pick firm and unblemished pods and serve this recipe chilled.

1 pound fresh Chinese peapods
1 cup water

DRESSING
1½ teaspoons sugar
½ teaspoon salt
⅛ teaspoon black pepper
1 tablespoon lite soy sauce
½ tablespoon sesame seed oil
1 teaspoon minced garlic

1. Mix the dressing ingredients in a small bowl and set aside.

2. Wash and snip off the top of each peapod. Place the peapods in a large microwave-safe dish and add the cup of water. Cover and microwave on high for 2½ minutes. Drain the peapods and refresh them in cold water to stop the cooking. Pat them dry.

3. Pour the dressing over the peapods and toss to mix well. Serve immediately or chill and serve.

PREPARATION TIME:	8-10 minutes
COOKING TIME:	2½ minutes
CHILLING TIME:	30 minutes
SERVES	4
MAKE AHEAD:	Yes

EACH SERVING: 70 Calories/ 16 Calories from Fat/ 23% Calories from Fat

White Rice

It is very easy to make boiled rice the Chinese way, from scratch. Master this technique and you will always enjoy fluffy rice. If you eat rice often, an electric rice cooker is a good investment. You are guaranteed a perfect pot of rice every time.

1 cup long grain white rice
1¾ cups cold water

1. Put the rice in a 1-quart saucepan and rinse it twice with cold water. Pour off the excess water by cupping your hand over the rice grains. *Do not use a colander.* Add the cold water and bring the rice to a boil, uncovered, over high heat.

2. When the water bubbles to the top of the saucepan in about 7 minutes, turn the heat to medium and continue cooking uncovered. Stir with a fork or chopsticks occasionally to prevent sticking.

3. After about 5 minutes, when the water is almost evaporated, reduce the heat to simmer. Cover the saucepan with a tight-fitting lid and steam for about 20 minutes. Do not lift the lid during this time.

4. When the steaming is complete, fluff the rice with a fork or chopsticks. Replace the lid and let the rice stand until you are ready to serve.

PREPARATION TIME:	*2 minutes*
COOKING TIME:	*32 minutes*
YIELD:	*3½ cups cooked rice*
SERVES:	*7 (½ cup per serving)*
NOTE:	*Use the following formula to cook more rice: 2 cups of rice to 2¾ cups of water, yields 7 cups cooked rice; 3 cups of rice to 3¾ cups of water, yields about 10 cups of cooked rice. To succeed with these proportions, the rice must be rinsed twice (so that it can absorb some water) and drained by pouring the water off the rice instead of using a colander. Cup your hand over the rice as you pour off the water. Use a larger saucepan for larger quantities and allow for longer cooking time.*

EACH SERVING: 113 Calories/ 0 Calories from Fat/ 0% Calories from Fat

week 4

Turkey Vegetable Soup

Here's a soup that nurtures the soul like mother's own chicken soup. All you need is turkey drumstick, together with carrots and Napa cabbage. Sweet and delicious, this soup can easily be made for a group by doubling the recipe.

a turkey drumstick, about 1½ pounds
a 1-inch knob of gingerroot
2 quarts + 2 quarts and 2 cups cold water
2 tablespoons dry white wine
2 large carrots
1 pound Napa cabbage
salt and pepper to taste

1. Wash the drumstick and pat it dry with paper towels. Set aside.

2. Bring 2 quarts of cold water to a boil in a 6-quart saucepan. Add the drumstick. Boil for 5 minutes. Drain and run cold water over the drumstick. Cut off the skin and trim any fat.

3. Add 2 quarts plus 2 cups of cold water to the saucepan. Put in the gingerroot and wine. Bring to a boil. Add the drumstick and bring the pot to a second boil. Cover and turn the heat to medium. Cook for 1½ hours.

4. While the soup is cooking, pare the carrots and cut them diagonally into 1/2-inch-wide slices. Set aside.

5. Wash the Napa cabbage and cut it into quarters, lengthwise. Then cut each quarter, crosswise, into 1-inch segments. Set aside.

6. After 1½ hours, remove the drumstick and add the vegetables to the cooking soup. Cover and cook for another 30 minutes.

7. Remove the turkey meat from the bones. Use the meat in a salad or with noodles, or chop the larger pieces and return them to the soup.

PREPARATION TIME: 20 minutes
COOKING TIME: 2 hours
SERVES: 9 (1 cup per serving)
NOTE: If you want the maximum flavor from the turkey, cook the soup 2 more hours
                      before removing the drumstick and adding the vegetables.

EACH SERVING WITH THE MEAT REMOVED:
27 Calories/ 1 Calories from Fat/ 3% Calories from Fat

EACH SERVING WITH MEAT:
96 Calories/ 23 Calories from Fat/ 23% Calories from Fat

Curried Shrimp on Bean Sprouts

The crunchy texture of fresh bean sprouts is delicately counterbalanced by the meaty shrimp texture and the pleasant bite of the curry. This is one of Donna's favorites!

1 pound medium shrimp in the shell
½ pound fresh bean sprouts
1 tablespoon oil
1 teaspoon minced garlic

MARINADE
1 teaspoon sugar
½ teaspoon cornstarch
¼ teaspoon salt
⅛ teaspoon black pepper
2 tablespoons dry white wine

CURRY SAUCE
2 tablespoons curry powder
1 teaspoon cornstarch
½ teaspoon sugar
¼ teaspoon black pepper
1 cup chicken broth
2 tablespoons 2% milk
1 tablespoon oyster-flavored sauce

GARNISH
2 tablespoons diced scallions

1. In a large bowl, mix the marinade ingredients until smooth and set aside.

2. Peel, wash and devein the shrimp. Pat them dry with paper towels. Add them to the marinade bowl. Stir well to evenly coat the shrimp and let stand for 30 minutes or longer.

3. Wash and drain the bean sprouts. Make a bed of sprouts on a serving platter and set aside.

4. Mix the curry sauce and set aside.

5. Heat a wok on high for 30 seconds. Add the oil and swirl to coat the wok for 30 seconds longer. Add the garlic and stir-toss for 10 seconds. Add the curry sauce, mix well, and bring to a quick boil. Add the shrimp with its marinade, stir-toss, and cook for 2 more minutes. Ladle the shrimp and sauce over the bean sprouts. Sprinkle the diced scallions on top and serve.

PREPARATION TIME: *20-25 minutes*
MARINATING TIME: *30 minutes*
COOKING TIME: *5 minutes*
SERVES: *4*

EACH SERVING: 164 Calories/ 46 Calories from Fat/ 28% Calories from Fat

Rice with a Tropical Flair

Bring Summer and sunshine into your meal with this tropical treat. Spiking the dish with vinegar gives it a sour bite that complements the sweet pineapple. I find this recipe a perfect way to use day-old rice. For a one-dish meal – simply add cooked chicken, steamed shrimp or leftover turkey.

2 cups day-old rice
4 egg whites, lightly beaten with 1 tablespoon Maggie seasoning
1 tablespoon oil
1 10-ounce can crushed pineapple in unsweetened juice, drained
1 tablespoon white vinegar
4 tablespoons diced scallions

1. Separate the rice clumps with your hands and set the rice aside.

2. Heat a wok on high for 1½ minutes. Add the oil and swirl to coat the work for 1½ minutes more until the wok is smoking. Pour in the egg white mixed with Maggie seasoning and stir quickly. Add the rice and stir-toss for 2 minutes. Add the pineapple. Stir-toss and mix for 1 minute. Add the vinegar and scallions and mix well with the rice. Turn the heat to medium, cover, and cook for 3 minutes.

3. Dish up the rice and serve hot.

PREPARATION TIME: Less than 5 minutes
COOKING TIME: 9 to 10 minutes
SERVES: 5 (¾ cup per serving)

EACH SERVING: 164 Calories/ 25 Calories from Fat/ 15% Calories from Fat

week

October

1	Chinese Turkey Patties Spinach & Mushrooms with Garlic Fragrant Rice
2	Poached Fish Fillets with Ginger & Scallions Chinese Broccoli & Straw Mushrooms Brown Rice
3	Sesame Sirloin Meatballs Stir-Tossed Cabbage with Ginger White Rice
4	Egg Drop & Spinach Soup Tofu Salad with Peapods & Peppers Rice with Crabmeat & Mushrooms

October week 1

Chinese Turkey Patties
Spinach & Mushrooms with Garlic
Fragrant Rice
284 Calories/ 45 Calories from Fat/ 16% Calories from Fat

Chinese Turkey Patties

This recipe offers a healthy and tasty alternative to beef hamburgers. The turkey patties, after a 30-minute marinating, can be broiled in a conventional oven, microwaved or grilled.

1 pound lean ground turkey
1 medium onion, diced
vegetable spray

SEASONING
1 tablespoon cornstarch
1 teaspoon sugar
½ teaspoon salt
¼ teaspoon black pepper
2 tablespoons cold water
1½ tablespoons oyster-flavored sauce
1 tablespoon whiskey
1 teaspoon minced garlic

1. In a large bowl, mix the seasoning ingredients until smooth. Add the ground turkey. Mix well and let stand for 30 minutes or longer.

2. Put the diced onion in a food processor and fine-chop for about 30 seconds, scraping down the sides occasionally with a rubber spatula. Add it to the turkey and mix well.

3. Preheat the oven on broil. Line a baking pan with aluminum foil. Coat the lined pan with a thin layer of nonfat vegetable spray and set aside.

4. After the turkey has seasoned for 30 minutes, scoop up ½ cup, shape it into a ball, then flatten it into a patty. Make four more patties. Place the turkey patties on the baking pan and the pan on the top oven rack.

5. Broil for 8 minutes. Turn the patties and broil for another 8 minutes. Serve with the noodles and vegetable.

PREPARATION TIME:	*8-10 minutes*
MARINATING TIME:	*30 minutes*
COOKING TIME:	*16 minutes*
SERVES:	*5*
VARIATION:	*Use the mixture to make 1-inch meatballs and broil them for 10 minutes. These little fellows make a great entree or delicious appetizers.*
NOTE:	*To microwave the patties, place them on a microwave-safe plate, cover with paper towels and cook on high for 5 to 6 minutes. To grill the patties, cook for about 4 to 5 minutes on each side.*

EACH SERVING: 128 Calories/ 21 Calories from Fat/ 17% Calories from Fat

Spinach & Mushrooms with Garlic

Fresh spinach and mushrooms, stir-tossed gently with a hint of garlic, are a vegetable lover's delight. This dish nicely complements any meat, poultry or seafood entree.

1 pound fresh spinach
10 large mushrooms
1 teaspoon oil
1 tablespoon minced garlic

SEASONING
½ teaspoon salt
½ teaspoon sugar
½ teaspoon cornstarch
⅛ teaspoon black pepper
½ cup chicken broth
1 tablespoon dry white wine

1. Trim off the spinach roots and break the leaves in two. Wash them at least 3 times. Drain and pat dry.

2. Clean the mushrooms and thin-slice across each cap and stem. Set aside.

3. In a medium bowl, mix the seasoning ingredients until smooth and set aside.

4. Heat a wok on high for 30 seconds. Add the oil and swirl for 30 seconds to coat the wok. Add the garlic and stir-toss for 15 seconds. Add the seasoning mixture and bring it to a quick boil. Add the mushrooms and stir-toss for 1 minute. Add the spinach and stir-toss for another minute. Cover and cook on medium heat for 3 minutes.

5. Ladle to serving dish with a slotted spoon. Discard any excess sauce.

PREPARATION TIME: *15-18 minutes*
COOKING TIME: *8 minutes*
SERVES: *4*

EACH SERVING: 57 Calories/ 16 Calories from Fat/ 28% Calories from Fat

Fragrant Rice

Using jasmine rice instead of regular long grain rice introduces a fragrance the Chinese call *Hsiang mi,* "fragrant rice." Our recipe sweetens the pot even more by adding celery, scallions and cilantro and using chicken broth instead of water.

1 cup jasmine rice
1 teaspoon oil
3 stalks of celery, diced (preferably stalks near the heart)
1½ cups chicken broth
2 tablespoons diced scallions
2 tablespoons minced cilantro or Chinese parsley
½ teaspoon freshly ground white pepper

1. Put the rice in a large bowl and rinse it twice in cold water. Pour off the excess water by cupping your hand over the rice grains. Do not use a colander. Set aside.

2. Heat a 2-quart saucepan, add the oil and swirl it for 15 seconds to coat the pan. Add the celery and stir-toss for 45 seconds. Add the chicken broth and bring it to a boil. Add the rice and bring the pot to a second boil. Boil until the broth bubbles to the top, about 3 minutes. Turn the heat to medium and continue cooking, uncovered. Stir occasionally to prevent sticking.

3. When the broth is mostly evaporated (after about 5 minutes) reduce the heat to simmer, cover the pot with a tight-fitting lid and steam for 20 minutes more. Do not lift the lid during this time.

4. When the steaming is complete, fluff the rice, mix in the scallions, cilantro and pepper, fluff again, and serve immediately.

PREPARATION TIME: *5 minutes*
COOKING TIME: *31 minutes*
SERVES: *8 (½ cup servings)*

EACH SERVING: 99 Calories/ 8 Calories from Fat/ 9% Calories from Fat

week 2

Poached Fish Fillet with Ginger & Scallions
Chinese Broccoli & Straw Mushrooms
Brown Rice
334 Calories/ 56 Calories from Fat/ 17% Calories from Fat

Poached Fish Fillets with Ginger & Scallions

Amazingly simple to prepare and yet incredibly delicious, this dish must be tried to be believed! Here's a little secret: pick the freshest fish you can find. Whether you use whitefish, salmon, pickerel, snapper, or scrod– your family will be delighted with this treat.

1 pound fresh fish fillet
2 quarts warm water
a 1-inch knob gingerroot

SAUCE
1 tablespoon oil
4 thin slices gingerroot, slivered
2 scallions with greens, slivered
2 tablespoons Maggie seasoning

1. Crush the ginger knob to release its full flavor. Add it to the warm water in a 4-quart pot and bring to a quick boil.

2. Rinse the fillet and pat it dry with paper towels. Cut it lengthwise into four pieces and set them aside.

3. Cut the scallions and gingerroot slices into thin slivers and set them aside.

4. When the ginger water comes to a boil, turn off the heat and add the fillet sections. Poach for about 3 minutes. Check to see if the fish has turned opaque and flakes easily. If some of the flesh is still transparent, poach for another minute. With a slotted spatula gently lift each section from the water, drain it well, and place it on a serving platter. Set the platter aside.

5. Heat the oil in a small saucepan. When it starts to smoke, turn off the heat and add the scallions and gingerroot. Stir-toss for 30 seconds. Add the Maggie seasoning. Stir, then spread the sauce over the fish. Serve immediately.

PREPARATION TIME: *6 to 8 minutes*
COOKING TIME: *10 to 11 minutes*
SERVES: *4*

EACH SERVING: 138 Calories/ 38 Calories from Fat/ 29% Calories from Fat

Chinese Broccoli & Straw Mushrooms

The Chinese love their greens – especially Chinese broccoli or *gai lan*. *Gai lan* is prized for its taste and crunchy texture. This classic dish, served at the best Chinese restaurants and roadside stands, is one of my favorites. Use the stalks (they are tender and tasty) as well as the leaves.

1½ pounds fresh Chinese broccoli
2 quarts of warm water
a 1-inch knob of gingerroot, smashed
2 tablespoons dry white wine
1 teaspoon sugar
1 8-ounce can tiny peeled straw mushrooms, drained

SAUCE
½ teaspoon sugar
½ teaspoon cornstarch
¼ cup chicken broth
2 tablespoons water from the mushrooms
2 tablespoons oyster-flavored sauce
½ tablespoon sesame seed oil

1. Bring the warm water, wine, sugar and gingerroot to a quick boil in a 6-quart covered saucepan.

2. Rinse and drain the *gai lan* without cutting or breaking the stalks and leaves. Set aside.

3. When the water comes to a boil, add the *gai lan* and cook, uncovered, for 4 to 5 minutes – until it turns

bright, vibrant green. Drain and arrange artistically on a large platter.

4. While the *gai lan* is cooking, mix the sauce ingredients in a large bowl, and add the straw mushrooms. Microwave on high for 2 minutes and then pour over the *gai lan*.

5. Delicious hot or cold.

PREPARATION TIME:	*Less than 5 minutes*
COOKING TIME:	*12 minutes*
MAKE AHEAD:	*Yes, serve cold.*
SERVES:	*6*

EACH SERVING: 80 Calories/ 13 Calories from Fat/ 16% Calories from Fat

Brown Rice

Brown rice has more bran and fiber and is also more nutritious than white rice. Its nutty taste and texture give t a distinctive appeal. The kernels need to be washed three times so they will absorb more water before cooking.

1 cup long grain brown rice
2 cups cold water

1. Place the rice in a 1-quart saucepan and rinse it three separate times with cold water. Pour off the excess water, cupping your hand over the rice grains. Do not use a colander. Add 2 cups of cold water to the rice and bring it to a boil, uncovered, over high heat.

2. When the water bubbles to the top of the saucepan, in about 10 minutes, turn the heat to medium and continue cooking uncovered. Stir the rice with chopsticks or a fork occasionally to prevent sticking.

3. After about 5 minutes when the water has almost evaporated, turn the heat to simmer. Cover the pot with a tight-fitting lid and steam for about 20 minutes. Do not lift the cover during this time.

4. When steaming is complete, fluff the rice with chopsticks. Let the rice stand, covered, until you are ready to serve.

PREPARATION TIME:	*2 minutes*
COOKING TIME:	*35 minutes*
YIELD:	*2½ cups of cooked rice*
SERVES:	*5 (½ cup per serving)*

EACH SERVING: 116 Calories/ 5 Calories from Fat/ 5% Calories from Fat

week 3

Sesame Sirloin Meatballs

A creative way to use sesame seeds and turn ground beef into a spectacular dish. These delicious treats may be served plain or with a dipping sauce like those used for Baked Prawns. *See Week 2 for May.*

¼ cup toasted sesame seeds
1 pound very lean ground sirloin
4 tablespoons diced scallions

SEASONING
2 tablespoons cornstarch
1 teaspoon sugar
½ teaspoon baking soda
½ teaspoon black pepper
2 tablespoons oyster-flavored sauce
1 tablespoon dry white wine

1. Spread toasted sesame seeds on a plate. Set aside.

2. In a large bowl, blend the seasoning ingredients until smooth. Add the ground beef, mix well and set aside. Let stand for 30 minutes or longer. Add the diced scallions and knead the mixture with your hands for 1 minute.

3. Scoop out about a teaspoon of meat and roll it into a 1-inch ball. Continue until you have used all the meat. You should have about 35 balls. Roll the meatballs in sesame seeds so they are well-coated. Set aside.

4. Line a cookie sheet with aluminum foil. Preheat the oven to 425 degrees. Bake the meatballs for 5 minutes. Turn and bake for another 5 minutes. Serve hot.

PREPARATION TIME: *10 minutes*
MARINATING TIME: *30 minutes*
COOKING TIME: *10 minutes*

SERVES: *8*
NOTES: *This is a wonderful appetizer.*

To make toasted sesame seeds, place raw seeds on a cookie sheet and bake in a 250-degree oven for 30 minutes. Store leftover seeds in an airtight jar.

EACH SERVING: 117 Calories/ 43 Calories from Fat/ 38% Calories from Fat*
*These figures do not include the dipping sauces.

Stir-Tossed Cabbage with Ginger

Delicious hot or cold, this dish lifts the lowly cabbage into elegance. Ginger root heightens the flavor and reduces the gaseous nature of the cabbage.

½ head medium-sized cabbage
1 small knob gingerroot
1 small onion
6 medium mushrooms
½ tablespoon oil
½ teaspoon salt

SEASONING
1 teaspoon sugar
½ teaspoon cornstarch
⅛ teaspoon black pepper
¼ cup chicken broth
2 tablespoons water
2 tablespoons lite soy sauce
1 tablespoon dry white wine

1. Mix the seasoning ingredients in a medium-sized bowl and set aside.

2. Rinse and core the cabbage. Cut 3-inch wedges and then slice each wedge crosswise into ¼-inch-wide strips. Set aside. Smash the gingerroot to release its flavor and set aside.

3. Peel and cut off the ends of the onion. Halve and thin-slice the onion with the grain. Set aside. Clean the mushrooms, thin-slice them through the cap and stem, and set them aside.

4. Heat a wok on high for 30 seconds. Add the oil and salt and swirl to coat the wok for 30 seconds longer. Add the gingerroot and stir-toss for 30 seconds. Add the onion slices and mushrooms. Stir-toss for 1 minute.

Add the cabbage and stir-toss for another minute. Add the seasoning mixture and stir-toss for 30 seconds. Cover the wok, lower the heat to medium-high and cook for 8 more minutes. Discard the gingerroot before serving.

PREPARATION TIME:	*10-12 minutes*
COOKING TIME:	*12 minutes*
SERVES:	*4*

EACH SERVING: 72 Calories/ 20 Calories from Fat/ 27% Calories from Fat

White Rice

It is very easy to make boiled rice the Chinese way, from scratch. Master this technique and you will always enjoy fluffy rice. If you eat rice often, an electric rice cooker is a good investment. You are guaranteed a perfect pot of rice every time.

1 cup long grain white rice
1¾ cups cold water

1. Put the rice in a 1-quart saucepan and rinse it twice with cold water. Pour off the excess water by cupping your hand over the rice grains. *Do not use a colander.* Add the cold water and bring the rice to a boil, uncovered, over high heat.

2. When the water bubbles to the top of the saucepan in about 7 minutes, turn the heat to medium and continue cooking uncovered. Stir with a fork or chopsticks occasionally to prevent sticking.

3. After about 5 minutes, when the water is almost evaporated, reduce the heat to simmer. Cover the saucepan with a tight-fitting lid and steam for about 20 minutes. Do not lift the lid during this time.

4. When the steaming is complete, fluff the rice with a fork or chopsticks. Replace the lid and let the rice stand until you are ready to serve.

PREPARATION TIME:	*2 minutes*
COOKING TIME:	*32 minutes*
YIELD:	*3½ cups cooked rice*
SERVES:	*7 (½ cup per serving)*
NOTE:	*Use the following formula to cook more rice: 2 cups of rice to 2¾ cups of water, yields 7 cups cooked rice; 3 cups of rice to 3¾ cups of water, yields about 10 cups of cooked rice. To succeed with these proportions, the rice must be rinsed twice (so that it can absorb some water) and drained by pouring the water off the rice instead of using a colander. Cup your hand over the rice as you pour*

off the water. Use larger saucepans for larger quantities and allow for longer cooking time.

EACH SERVING: 113 Calories/ 0 Calories from Fat/ 0% Calories from Fat

week 4

Egg Drop & Spinach Soup
Tofu Salad with Peapods & Peppers
Rice with Crabmeat & Mushrooms
316 Calories/ 55 Calories from Fat/ 17% Calories from Fat

Egg Drop & Spinach Soup

Sometimes I prefer the sheer simplicity of an all-time favorite. This gentle soup is unbeatable.

5 cups chicken stock
10-ounces frozen chopped spinach, thawed
3 egg whites, lightly beaten

GARNISH
2 tablespoons diced scallions

1. Place the chicken stock and spinach in a 4-quart saucepan. Cover, and bring to a boil in about 9 minutes. Turn the heat to medium-high and continue cooking for 2 more minutes.

2. Turn off the heat and slowly drizzle in the egg whites. Ladle to soup bowls and garnish each bowl with diced scallions.

PREPARATION TIME:	*2-3 minutes*
COOKING TIME:	*11 minutes*
SERVES:	*6*
VARIATION:	*Add a cup of diced chicken for a soup of "more substance."*

EACH SERVING: 47 Calories/ 9 Calories from Fat/ 18% Calories from Fat

Tofu Salad with Peapods & Peppers

Simple to make but rich in taste, this recipe is almost too good to be true. It can be served at room temperature or chilled to serve later.

¼ pound fresh peapods
2 cups boiling water
1 10½-ounce package Mori-Nu extra-firm lite tofu, drained
½ yellow or sweet red pepper
2 tablespoons diced scallions
1 teaspoon minced garlic

DRESSING
½ teaspoon cornstarch
½ teaspoon sugar
⅛ teaspoon white pepper
2 tablespoons oyster-flavored sauce
2 tablespoons cold water
½ tablespoon sesame seed oil
½ tablespoon cider vinegar

1. Wash the peapods and snip off the tops. Cut each peapod crosswise into ½-inch pieces. Soak in 2 cups of boiling water for 1 minute. Drain and set aside.

2. Cut the tofu into ½-inch cubes and drain again. Set aside.

3. Trim the pepper, cut it in half and clean out the seeds. Cut ½-inch cubes and set aside.

4. Mix the dressing ingredients in a large microwave-safe bowl. Cover and microwave on high for 1 minute. Add the tofu and blend well. Add the peapods and pepper cubes. Mix well, then add the scallions and garlic and toss again. Serve immediately or chill to serve later.

PREPARATION TIME:	*12-15 minutes*
SOAKING TIME:	*1 minute*
COOKING TIME:	*1 minute*
SERVES:	*5*
NOTE:	*Mori-Nu lite tofu is truly low-fat – only 1% fat per serving. Other kinds of tofu have much high fat content. The extra-firm variety has more texture.*

EACH SERVING: 65 Calories/ 20 Calories from Fat/ 30% Calories from Fat

Rice with Crabmeat & Mushrooms

This dish is a great crowd-pleaser and my 7-year-old grandson's favorite. In fact, I created it especially for him. Around out house it's called "Ian's Rice Recipe"! *Note that this recipe presumes you have already cooked a pot of white rice and have it ready!*

6 ounces of crab meat
6 medium mushrooms
1 small onion
4 medium-sized fresh asparagus spears

SEASONING
¼ tablespoon cornstarch
½ tablespoon cold water
¼ teaspoon salt
dash of white pepper
½ tablespoon Maggi seasoning
½ tablespoon dry white wine
6 tablespoons chicken broth
6 tablespoons 2% milk

½ tablespoon oil
2 cups freshly-cooked hot rice

1. Cut the crab into 1-inch pieces. Set aside.

2. Clean the mushrooms and trim the stems to ½ inch from the cap. Thin-slice through cap and stem and set aside.

3. Trim and peel the onion. Halve and thin-slice it with the grain. Set aside.

4. Snap off and discard the tough end of each asparagus spear. (If you bend the stalk using both hands, it will usually break at the woody part of the stem.) Wash, drain, and thin-slice the spears diagonally into ½-inch pieces. Set aside.

5. In a large bowl, mix the cornstarch with cold water, blending until smooth. Add the other ingredients for the seasoning, mix well and set aside.

6. Heat a wok on high for 30 seconds. Add the oil and swirl to coat the sides of the wok for 30 seconds. Add the onion and stir-toss for 30 seconds. Add the mushrooms and stir-toss for 30 seconds. Add the asparagus and stir-toss for 30 seconds. Add the seasoning mixture and bring to a boil. Add the crab meat, cover and cook for 2 minutes.

7. Dish up the hot rice, top it with the crab and vegetable mixture and serve immediately.

PREPARATION TIME:	*10-12 minutes*
COOKING TIME:	*5½ minutes*
SERVES:	*4*
NOTE:	*Imitation crab can be used in this recipe.*

EACH SERVING: 204 Calories/ 26 Calories from Fat/ 13% Calories from Fat

week November

1	Sichuan Chicken Bean Sprouts Fit for a King Noodles with Onion & Tomato Sauce
2	Sweet & Sour Fish Peapod, Egg, Tomato & Mushroom Salad Brown Rice
3	Baked Gourmet Beef Patties Shanghai String Bean Salad Fragrant Rice
4	Scallops & Shrimp with Hoisin Sauce Eggplant in Savory Sauce White Rice

November week 1

Sichuan Chicken
Bean Sprouts Fit for a King
Noodles with Onion & Tomato Sauce
328 Calories/ 69 Calories from Fat/ 21% Calories from Fat

Sichuan Chicken

Delicious baked or grilled, this spicy, plan-ahead dish is well worth the 2-hour marinating time.

4 *4-ounce chicken thighs, skinned and boned*
            OR
2 *8-ounce chicken breasts, skinned and boned*

MARINADE
2 teaspoons sugar
1 teaspoon cornstarch
¼ teaspoon baking soda
¼ teaspoon black pepper
1½ cups cold water
2 tablespoons dry white wine
1½ tablespoons Hunan chili paste
1½ tablespoons oyster-flavored sauce
2 tablespoons scallions, diced
1 teaspoon garlic, minced
½ teaspoon gingerroot, grated

1. Wash the chicken, remove all fat, pat dry with paper towels. Set aside.

2. In a large bowl, mix the marinade and add the chicken. Refrigerate for two hours or more. Turn the meat occasionally to assure that the seasoning penetrates all the flesh.

3. When the chicken is almost through marinating, preheat the oven to 375 degrees. Line a baking pan with foil and put the chicken and its marinade in it. Bake for 25 minutes; turn it over and continue baking for another 20 minutes. Baste the chicken as you turn it.

4. Remove the chicken to a serving platter and top with any sauce left in the baking pan. Serve hot.

PREPARATION TIME: 12 minutes
MARINATING TIME: 2 hours
COOKING TIME: 45 minutes
SERVES: 4
NOTE: Use more or less Hunan chili paste to make the dish more or less spicy: fiery hot is 2 to 3 tablespoons; medium hot, 1 to 1½; and mild, ½ to ¾. Different brands also vary in intensity. Experiment for best results – and remember, it is much easier to add more chili paste than it is to cook more noodles, so begin with a mild mix!

*EACH SERVING WITH **WHITE** MEAT:*
159 Calories/ 14 Calories from Fat/9% Calories from Fat

*EACH SERVING WITH **DARK** MEAT:*
139 Calories/ 31 Calories from Fat/ 23% Calories from Fat

Bean Sprouts Fit for a King

The tangy taste of peppers, garlic and scallions turns "lowly" bean sprouts into a dish fit for a king. For a even greater visual treat, try using a kaleidoscopic combination of red, yellow and green peppers.

1 pound fresh bean sprouts
1 large green pepper
2 scallions with green tops
½ tablespoon oil
1 teaspoon minced garlic
1 tablespoon Maggi seasoning

SEASONING
1 teaspoon sugar

½ teaspoon salt
½ teaspoon cornstarch
⅛ teaspoon freshly ground white pepper
½ cup chicken broth
1 tablespoon dry white wine

1. Wash and drain the bean sprouts. Set them aside. Wash and halve the green pepper. Cut off and discard top, core and seeds. Cut each half into 3 pieces, lengthwise. Thin-slice each length crosswise into ⅛-inch wide pieces. Set aside.

2. Trim the roots off the scallions. Wash, pat dry, and cut them diagonally into fine slivers .

3. Mix seasoning ingredients in a small bowl and set aside.

4. Heat a wok on high for 30 seconds. Add the oil and swirl to coat the wok for 30 seconds longer. Add the minced garlic and stir-toss for 15 seconds. Add the seasoning mixture and bring it to a boil. Add the green pepper strips and stir-toss for 30 seconds. Add the bean sprouts, stir-toss, and cook for 1 minute. Add the scallions, cover, and cook for 1 minute. Uncover, stir-toss, cover, and cook for another minute.

5. *Just before dishing up,* add the Maggi seasoning, mixing it well with the vegetables. Ladle to a dish and serve hot.

PREPARATION TIME:	*6-8 minutes*
COOKING TIME:	*6 minutes*
SERVES:	*6*
NOTE:	*For a totally vegetarian presentation, use vegetable broth.*

EACH SERVING: 58 Calories/ 14 Calories from Fat/ 23% Calories from Fat

Noodles with Onion & Tomato Sauce

I love the look and taste of this simple noodle recipe. Only three ingredients! This dish can also serve as an entree – simply add cooked shrimp or cooked chunks of chicken, turkey or steak.

¼ pound thin dry noodles or vermicelli
8 cups cold water
1 large onion
2 cups boiling water
2 large tomatoes
1 tablespoon oil

SAUCE
½ tablespoon cornstarch
1 teaspoon sugar
¼ teaspoon black pepper
¼ cup + 2 tablespoons ketchup
2 tablespoons chicken broth
1 tablespoon dry white wine

1. Bring the water to a rolling boil in a 4-quart saucepan. Add the noodles and cook, uncovered, for about 7 minutes – until they are tender to the bite.

2. While the noodles are cooking, peel the onion and slice it with the grain into thin strips. Set aside.

3. In a medium-sized bowl, soak the tomatoes in 2 cups of boiling water for 1 minute. Drain them and, using a paring knife, gently remove the skin. Quarter the peeled tomatoes and then crosscut each quarter into small pieces. Set aside in a small bowl.

4. Mix the sauce in a medium-sized bowl and set it aside.

5. When the noodles are done, rinse them in cold water, drain, and transfer them to a large serving bowl. Set aside.

6. Heat a wok on high for 30 seconds. Add the oil and swirl to coat the wok for 30 seconds. Add the onion and stir-toss for 1 minute. Add the tomatoes and stir-toss for another minute. Add the sauce and bring it to a boil. Cook 1 minute longer. Pour the sauce over the noodles and serve.

PREPARATION TIME:	*8 to 10 minutes*
COOKING TIME:	*18 minutes*
SERVES:	*6 (2/3 cup per serving)*
NOTE:	*When using as an entree, you might wish to double the recipe.*

EACH SERVING: 131 Calories/ 24 Calories from Fat/ 18% Calories from Fat

week 2

Sweet & Sour Fish
Peapod, Egg, Tomato & Mushroom Salad
Brown Rice
434 Calories/ 83 Calories from Fat/ 19% Calories from Fat

Sweet & Sour Fish

Poaching fish is a viable alternative to steaming and produces an equally tender texture so important to the Chinese. The poaching time may be extended to 25 or 30 minutes without damaging the texture. To cook the fish whole, you will need a Dutch oven large enough to hold the fish on a heatproof platter.

1 whole fish, head, tail and fins intact
a 1½-inch knob of gingerroot
2 quarts warm water
½ small cucumber
½ small sweet red pepper
½ small onion
1 tablespoon oil

SAUCE
1½ tablespoons sugar
1 teaspoon cornstarch
⅛ teaspoon black pepper
¾ cup chicken broth
3 tablespoons wine vinegar
2 tablespoons dry white wine
2 tablespoons ketchup

1. Get your Dutch oven and fish platter ready. Make sure the platter can hold the entire fish and still fit into the Dutch oven.

2. Rinse the fish and pat it dry with paper towels. Make several crosswise cuts about 1-inch apart and ½-inch deep on each side. Place the fish on the platter. Set aside.

3. Put the warm water in the Dutch oven. Smash the gingerroot flat to release its flavor. Add it to the Dutch oven and bring the water to a quick boil over high heat. Turn off the heat. Place the fish platter in the Dutch oven so that the water covers it. *Do not cover the Dutch oven.* Let the fish sit for 18 to 20 minutes. Since the heat is turned off and the pot is not covered, the fish will not overcook, even if it sits in the water for an extra 5 minutes.

4. Peel and thin-slice the onion with the grain. Thin-slice the red pepper and cucumber into match sticks. Set aside.

5. In a medium-sized bowl, blend the sauce ingredients until smooth and set aside.

6. Minutes before you are ready to serve, heat a wok on high for 30 seconds. Add the oil and swirl to coat the wok evenly for 30 seconds. Add the onion. Stir-toss for 30 seconds. Add the red pepper and cucumber sticks. Stir-toss for 30 seconds longer. Add the sauce and bring to a quick boil. Set aside.

7. Carefully pour off the poaching liquid and gently remove the fish from the plate using slotted spatulas. Drain it well. Turn the fish bottom side up as you place it on the serving platter.

8. Ladle the sweet and sour sauce over it and serve immediately.

PREPARATION TIME:	*8-10 minutes*
POACHING TIME:	*18-20 minutes*
SERVES:	*4*
EQUIPMENT:	*A Dutch oven, a large heatproof platter, and two very long slotted spatulas.*
NOTE:	*Pickerel, whitefish and bass are delicious prepared this way.*

EACH SERVING: 219 Calories/ 60 Calories from Fat/ 28% Calories from Fat

Peapod, Egg, Tomato & Mushroom Salad

An unusual combination, but unrivaled in taste, color and presentation. A winner every time!

8 medium dried black Chinese mushrooms
1 cup warm water
12 ounces fresh Chinese peapods
1 cup cold water
4 small firm tomatoes
4 hard-boiled eggs, whites only

MARINADE
½ teaspoon sugar
⅛ teaspoon black pepper
¼ cup cold water
1 tablespoon oyster-flavored sauce
½ tablespoon dry white wine
½ tablespoon sesame seed oil

1. Mix the marinade ingredients in a small bowl and set aside. Chill the salad plates in the refrigerator.

2. Place the dried black Chinese mushrooms, caps down, in a microwave-safe bowl with 1 cup of warm water. Cover and microwave on high for 5 minutes. Drain the mushrooms, refresh them in cold water and squeeze them dry. Remove and discard the stems. Thin-slice the caps. Return them to the microwave bowl. Add the marinade mixture, blend well, cover, and microwave on high for 4 minutes. Mix well and set aside.

3. Wash and drain the peapods. Snip off the tops. Place the peapods in a large microwave-safe dish and add 1 cup of cold water. Cover and microwave on high for 3 minutes. Drain the peapods and refresh them with cold

water to stop the cooking. Drain them again and pat them dry. Divide the peapods into 4 equal portions.

4. Halve the tomatoes and cut each half into 3 wedges. Set aside. Quarter the hard-boiled eggs and discard the yolks. Halve each quarter and set aside.

5. Arrange the peapods like a sunburst on individual pre-chilled salad plates. Add the tomato wedges and egg in alternate patterns. Place ¼ portion of the Chinese mushrooms and marinade in the center of each plate.

6. Serve as is or add a salad dressing of your choice.

PREPARATION TIME:	*12-15 minutes*
COOKING TIME:	*12 minutes*
SERVES:	*4*
MAKE AHEAD:	*Yes*

EACH SERVING: 99 Calories/ 18 Calories from Fat/ 18% Calories from Fat

Brown Rice

Brown rice has more bran and fiber and is also more nutritious than white rice. Its nutty taste and texture give it a distinctive appeal. The kernels need to be washed three times so they will absorb more water before cooking.

1 cup long grain brown rice
2 cups cold water

1. Place the rice in a 1-quart saucepan and rinse it three separate times with cold water. Pour off the excess water, cupping your hand over the rice grains. Do not use a colander. Add 2 cups of cold water to the rice and bring it to a boil, uncovered, over high heat.

2. When the water bubbles to the top of the saucepan, in about 10 minutes, turn the heat to medium and continue cooking uncovered. Stir the rice with chopsticks or a fork occasionally to prevent sticking.

3. After about 5 minutes when the water has almost evaporated, turn the heat to simmer. Cover the pot with a tight-fitting lid and steam for about 20 minutes. Do not lift the cover during this time.

4. When steaming is complete, fluff the rice with chopsticks. Let the rice stand, covered, until you are ready to serve.

PREPARATION TIME:	*2 minutes*
COOKING TIME:	*35 minutes*
YIELD:	*2½ cups of cooked rice*
SERVES:	*5 (½ cup per serving)*

EACH SERVING: 116 Calories/ 5 Calories from Fat/ 5% Calories from Fat

week 3

Baked Gourmet Beef Patties

These meat patties are extraordinary – worthy of your most important guests. The seasoning and water chestnuts add a unique flavor and crunch. In addition to serving these patties with the noodles offered in this meal, try them on rice, pasta or hamburger buns.

1 pound very lean ground sirloin
12 canned water chestnuts, finely chopped

SEASONING
1 tablespoon cornstarch
1 teaspoon sugar
¼ teaspoon baking soda
¼ teaspoon black pepper
1 tablespoon lite soy sauce
1 tablespoon dry white wine
1 tablespoon oyster-flavored sauce
1 tablespoon cold water
1 teaspoon minced garlic
2 tablespoons diced scallions

1. In a large bowl, mix the marinade until smooth. Add the ground beef and mix well. Let stand for 30 minutes or longer. Add the chopped water chestnuts. Knead the beef mixture with your hands for 1 minute. Make 6 patties. Set aside.

2. Move the oven rack to about 4½ inches from the heat. Preheat the oven to 425 degrees. Line a cookie sheet with foil. Place the patties on the cookie sheet. For a medium-well-done patty, bake for 7 minutes, turn and bake for 7 more minutes. Increase or decrease the time by a couple of minutes on each side for well-done or rare patties.

3. Serve hot out of the oven.

PREPARATION TIME:	8-10 minutes
MARINATING TIME:	30 minutes
COOKING TIME:	14 minutes
SERVES:	6

EACH SERVING: 127 Calories/ 34 Calories from Fat/ 28% Calories from Fat

Shanghai String Bean Salad

A fail-proof recipe for fresh green beans. For maximum flavor, prepare this dish the day before.

1 pound fresh green beans
2 quarts cold water

DRESSING
½ teaspoon sugar
⅛ teaspoon black pepper
2 tablespoons wine vinegar
2 tablespoons Maggi seasoning
½ tablespoon sesame seed oil
1 teaspoon minced garlic

1. Place the cold water in a large saucepan with a lid and bring to a boil, in about 5 minutes. While the water is boiling, snip off the ends of the beans with a pair of kitchen shears. Wash, drain and set them aside.

2. Mix the dressing ingredients in a large bowl and set aside.

3. When the water is boiling, add the beans, cover and cook on high for 5 minutes. Drain and refresh them in cold water to stop the cooking. Add the beans to the bowl with the dressing. Toss to coat them well. Refrigerate, covered, for an hour or overnight. Tossing the beans from time to time helps the dressing seep into the beans.

PREPARATION TIME:	6-8 minutes
COOKING TIME:	10 minutes
REFRIGERATION:	1 hour or overnight
SERVES:	4

EACH SERVING: 64 Calories/ 17 Calories from Fat/ 25% Calories from Fat

Fragrant Rice

Using jasmine rice instead of regular long grain rice introduces a fragrance the Chinese call *Hsiang mi,* "fragrant rice." Our recipe sweetens the pot even more by adding celery, scallions and cilantro and using chicken broth instead of water.

1 cup jasmine rice
1 teaspoon oil
3 stalks of celery, diced (preferably stalks near the heart)
1½ cups chicken broth
2 tablespoons diced scallions
2 tablespoons minced cilantro or Chinese parsley
½ teaspoon freshly ground white pepper

1. Put the rice in a large bowl and rinse it twice in cold water. Pour off the excess water by cupping your hand over the rice grains. Do not use a colander. Set aside.

2. Heat a 2-quart saucepan, add the oil and swirl it for 15 seconds to coat the pan. Add the celery and stir-toss for 45 seconds. Add the chicken broth and bring it to a boil. Add the rice and bring the pot to a second boil. Boil until the broth bubbles to the top, about 3 minutes. Turn the heat to medium and continue cooking, uncovered. Stir occasionally to prevent sticking.

3. When the broth is mostly evaporated (after about 5 minutes) reduce the heat to simmer, cover the pot with a tight-fitting lid and steam for 20 minutes more. Do not lift the lid during this time.

4. When the steaming is complete, fluff the rice, mix in the scallions, cilantro and pepper, fluff again, and serve immediately.

PREPARATION TIME: *5 minutes*
COOKING TIME: *31 minutes*
SERVES: *8 (½ cup servings)*

EACH SERVING: 99 Calories/ 8 Calories from Fat/ 9% Calories from Fat

week 4

Scallops & Shrimp with Hoisin Sauce
Eggplant in Savory Sauce
White Rice
338 Calories/ 59 Calories from Fat/ 17% Calories from Fat

Scallops & Shrimp with Hoisin Sauce

This recipe brings out the true sweetness of fresh scallops and shrimp. Gently poaching the seafood cooks it to perfection. The hoisin sauce is a delicate complement.

½ pound sea scallops
½ pound large shrimp in the shell, about 12 or 13

POACHING LIQUID
2 quarts warm water
4 tablespoons diced scallions
1 teaspoon grated gingerroot
1 teaspoon minced garlic

SAUCE
1 teaspoon sugar
1 teaspoon cornstarch
¼ teaspoon black pepper
½ cup chicken broth
2 tablespoons hoisin sauce
2 tablespoons ketchup
1 tablespoon oyster-flavored sauce
1 tablespoon dry white wine

SEASONING
1 tablespoon oil (to coat wok)
2 tablespoons diced scallions
a 1-inch knob fresh gingerroot
1 tablespoon whiskey

1. Bring the 2 quarts of warm water to a quick boil in a 4-quart covered saucepan. Add the scallions, ginger root and garlic for poaching. Bring it to a second boil in about 1 minute. Turn off the heat.

2. Rinse the scallops and pat them dry with paper towels. Halve each scallop into two rounds of equal thickness and set aside.

3. Peel the shrimp *but leave the tail shell on.* Make a ¼-inch-deep cut along the back of each shrimp to butterfly it. Devein and rinse them. Pat them dry with paper towels and set them aside.

4. In a medium-sized bowl, mix the sauce and set aside.

5. Turn on the heat under the poaching liquid and bring it to a quick boil. Turn off the heat again and remove the pan from the stove. Add the scallops and shrimp. Cover and let stand for 2 minutes. With a slotted spoon, remove the scallops and shrimp, drain and place them on a serving platter. Set aside.

6. Heat a wok on high for 30 seconds. Add the oil and swirl to coat the wok for 30 seconds. Add the other seasoning ingredients. Stir-toss for 15 seconds. Add the sauce and bring the mixture to a quick boil. Continue cooking for 1 more minute.

7. Drain the seafood again to remove any residual water from the serving platter. Ladle the sauce over the seafood and serve.

PREPARATION TIME: *12-15 minutes*
COOKING TIME: *11 minutes*
SERVES: *4*

EACH SERVING: 153 Calories/ 41 Calories from Fat/ 28% Calories from Fat

Eggplant in Savory Sauce

If you have never cooked eggplant before, this recipe will make a eggplant convert of you! Simple, but luscious, this versatile recipe can be made ahead of time and reheated – or served cold.

1 large eggplant
8 medium-sized fresh mushrooms
½ cup chicken broth

SAUCE
1½ teaspoons sugar
¼ teaspoon black pepper
1 tablespoon wine vinegar

1 tablespoon lite soy sauce
1 tablespoon oyster-flavored sauce
½ tablespoon sesame seed oil
½ teaspoon minced garlic

1. Wash the eggplant but do not peel it. Cut off the top and quarter it lengthwise. Cut across each quarter to make ¼-inch-thick slices. Place the slices in a microwave-safe dish with a cover. Set aside.

2. Clean the mushrooms and trim the stems if necessary. Thin-slice through each mushroom cap and stem, making ¼-inch thick slices. Add the mushrooms to the eggplant. Pour in the broth, cover the dish, and microwave it on high for 10 minutes. Stir the vegetables, cover, and microwave on high for another 10 minutes.

3. While the dish is cooking, mix the sauce ingredients in a small covered jar and shake to blend. When the vegetables are done, add the sauce and toss the mixture with a fork until it is well-blended. Serve with the rice.

PREPARATION TIME:	*5-8 minutes*
COOKING TIME:	*20 minutes*
SERVES:	*4*
VARIATIONS:	*For a spicy Sichuan flavor, add 1 to 2 tablespoons of Hunan chili paste to the sauce.*

EACH SERVING: 72 Calories/ 18 Calories from Fat/ 25% Calories from Fat

White Rice

It is very easy to make boiled rice the Chinese way, from scratch. Master this technique and you will always enjoy fluffy rice. If you eat rice often, an electric rice cooker is a good investment. You are guaranteed a perfect pot of rice every time.

1 cup long grain white rice
1¾ cups cold water

1. Put the rice in a 1-quart saucepan and rinse it twice with cold water. Pour off the excess water by cupping your hand over the rice grains. *Do not use a colander.* Add the cold water and bring the rice to a boil, uncovered, over high heat.

2. When the water bubbles to the top of the saucepan in about 7 minutes, turn the heat to medium and continue cooking uncovered. Stir with a fork or chopsticks occasionally to prevent sticking.

3. After about 5 minutes, when the water is almost evaporated, reduce the heat to simmer. Cover the saucepan with a tight-fitting lid and steam for about 20 minutes. Do not lift the lid during this time.

4. When the steaming is complete, fluff the rice with a fork or chopsticks. Replace the lid and let the rice stand until you are ready to serve.

PREPARATION TIME: *2 minutes*
COOKING TIME: *32 minutes*
YIELD: *3½ cups cooked rice*
SERVES: *7 (½ cup per serving)*
NOTE: *Use the following formula to cook more rice: 2 cups of rice to 2¾ cups of water, yields 7 cups cooked rice; 3 cups of rice to 3¾ cups of water, yields about 10 cups of cooked rice. To succeed with these proportions, the rice must be rinsed twice (so that it can absorb some water) and drained by pouring the water off the rice instead of using a colander. Cup your hand over the rice as you pour off the water. Use larger saucepans for larger quantities and allow for longer cooking time.*

EACH SERVING: 113 Calories/ 0 Calories from Fat/ 0% Calories from Fat

week

December

1	Chicken Fingers Ivory & Jade Flowers Sesame Noodles
2	Salmon Fillets with Hunan Chili Paste Stir-Tossed Potato & Carrot Sticks White Rice
3	Roasted Pork Chops Chinese Tossed Salad Noodles in Broth
4	Braised Lamb with Leeks Green Bean & Water Chestnut Salad Fragrant Rice

December week 1

Chicken Fingers
Ivory & Jade Flowers
Sesame Noodles
286 Calories/ 73 Calories from Fat/ 26% Calories from Fat

Chicken Fingers

You can quickly prepare this all-time favorite right in your own kitchen – even when your pantry is skimpy. Chicken fingers make a great entree and a delicious appetizer.

1 8-ounce chicken breast
1 egg white
2 tablespoons toasted sesame seeds
vegetable oil spray

MARINADE
2 teaspoons cornstarch
½ teaspoon sugar
¼ teaspoon salt
¼ teaspoon baking soda
¼ teaspoon white pepper
1 tablespoon dry white wine
½ teaspoon oyster-flavored sauce

1. Mix the marinade ingredients in a medium-sized bowl and set aside.

2. Remove all skin and fat from the chicken breast. Cut it into strips, 2 inches long and ¼ inch wide, making about 26 strips. Place the strips in the marinade bowl. Marinate them for 30 minutes or longer.

3. Lightly spray the surface of a baking sheet with vegetable oil. Preheat the oven to 375 degrees.

4. Beat the egg white in a chilled metal bowl until frothy. Add the sesame seeds and set aside.

5. After the chicken has marinated for at least 30 minutes, add the egg white and sesame seed mixture. Stir well to coat the strips. Place the strips side by side on the baking sheet. Bake the strips for 5 minutes. Turn them over and continue baking for another 3 minutes.

6. Cool the Chicken Fingers for 5 minutes before removing them to a serving platter.

PREPARATION TIME:	*8-10 minutes*
MARINATING TIME:	*30 minutes*
COOKING TIME:	*8 minutes*
COOLING TIME:	*5 minutes*
SERVES:	*4*
NOTE:	*To make toasted sesame seeds, place raw seeds on a cookie sheet and bake in a 250-degree oven for 30 minutes. Store leftover toasted seeds in an airtight container.*

EACH SERVING: 100 Calories/ 24 Calories from Fat/ 24% Calories from Fat

Ivory & Jade Flowers

Stir-tossed and flavored with garlic and oyster sauce, these vegetables are simply scrumptious. This is one of Donna's favorite recipes. Try to stop at just one helping.

½ large head cauliflower
1 stalk broccoli
½ tablespoon oil
1 teaspoon minced garlic
½ teaspoon salt

SEASONING
1 teaspoon sugar
½ teaspoon cornstarch
¼ teaspoon black pepper
2 tablespoons chicken broth

2 tablespoons water
1 tablespoon oyster-flavored sauce
1 tablespoon dry white wine

1. Rinse the cauliflower. Remove and discard the leaves and cut off about 1 inch of the stem. Separate flowerets and cut them into 2-inch long pieces. Half or quarter the thicker pieces.

2. Rinse the broccoli and cut the flowerets into 2-inch lengths. Peel the broccoli stalk with a paring knife. Slice the stalk into ½-inch diagonal slices or roll-cut it into 2-inch lengths. Set aside.

3. Mix the seasoning ingredients in a medium-sized bowl and set aside.

4. Heat a wok on high for 30 seconds. Add the oil and swirl to coat the wok for 30 seconds longer. Add the garlic and salt. Stir-toss for 15 seconds. Add the cauliflower. Stir-toss for 1 minute. Add the broccoli and stir-toss for 1 more minute. Pour in the seasoning mixture, blend well, cover, and cook for 3 minutes longer. This dish may be served hot or cold.

PREPARATION TIME: *8-10 minutes*
COOKING TIME: *7 minutes*
SERVES: *4*

EACH SERVING: 74 Calories/ 20 Calories from Fat/ 25% Calories from Fat

Sesame Noodles

My low-calorie version of a traditional Beijing favorite. Roadside stands and fine restaurants alike boast of their special sesame noodles recipes. Try mine!

2 quarts cold water
¼ pound thin dry noodles or vermicelli
1 large scallion
1 small carrot
1 tablespoon water
1 tablespoon toasted sesame seeds

DRESSING
½ teaspoon sugar
¼ teaspoon salt
¼ teaspoon black pepper
1 tablespoon cider vinegar

1 tablespoon lite soy sauce
1 tablespoon sesame seed oil
1 teaspoon minced garlic

1. Bring 2 quarts of water to a rolling boil in a 4-quart saucepan. Add the vermicelli and cook, uncovered, for about 7 minutes – until they are tender to the bite.

2. While the noodles are cooking, fine-cut the carrot. Place the carrot slivers in a microwave-safe dish with 1 tablespoon of cold water and cook, covered, on high for 1 minute. Pour out the water and set the carrots aside. Fine-cut the scallion into slivers and set aside.

3. Drain the noodles in a colander under cold running water. Transfer them to a large bowl. Blend the dressing ingredients by shaking them in a small covered jar and pour this mixture over the noodles. Mix well, then add the toasted sesame seeds (see note below) and mix again. Garnish with the scallion and carrot slivers. Delicious hot or cold.

PREPARATION TIME:	*5-10 minutes*
COOKING TIME:	*12-15 minutes*
YIELD:	*3 cups cooked noodles*
SERVES:	*6 (½ cup per serving)*
NOTE:	*Sesame seeds need to be toasted to bring out their sweet, nutlike flavor. Spread the seeds on a cookie sheet and bake them for 30 minutes in a 250-degree oven. Toasted seeds can be stored in an airtight covered jar for weeks – ready to use in other dishes.*
MAKE AHEAD:	*Yes, serve chilled.*

EACH SERVING: 112 Calories/ 29 Calories from Fat/ 26% Calories from Fat

week 2

Salmon Fillets with Hunan Chili Paste
Stir-Tossed Potato & Carrot Sticks
White Rice
519 Calories/ 109 Calories from Fat/ 21% Calories from Fat

Salmon Fillets with Hunan Chili Paste

Rich and scrumptious, yet amazingly simple. A chef's recipe that you can serve with pride. Sichuan/Hunan food aficionados *love* this dish and will bribe you for the recipe.

4 4-ounce salmon fillets
2 quarts warm water
a 1-inch knob fresh gingerroot

SAUCE
1 teaspoon oil*
4 tablespoons diced scallions*
1 teaspoon grated gingerroot*
     * Keep the 3 items above separate from the following:
1 teaspoon sugar
1 teaspoon cornstarch
½ cup chicken broth
2 tablespoons Hunan chili paste
1 tablespoon oyster-flavored sauce
1 tablespoon whiskey

1. In a medium-sized bowl, mix the last 6 sauce ingredients until smooth. Set aside.

2. Rinse the salmon fillets and pat them dry with paper towels. Set them aside.

3. Put the warm water in a large saucepan with a lid. Smash the gingerroot knob flat to release its full flavor and add it to the saucepan. Cover and bring the water to a quick boil on high heat. Add the salmon. Cover and remove the saucepan from the heat to continue poaching the salmon.

4. The fillets should be done in about 3 minutes. Test to see if they have turned opaque and flake easily when touched with a fork. Carefully drain the fish fillets (they will be fragile) using a slotted spoon or spatula as you transfer them to a serving platter. Set aside.

5. To prepare the sauce, heat a wok on high for 30 seconds. Add the oil and swirl to evenly coat the wok for 30 seconds. Add the scallions and gingerroot and stir-toss for 30 seconds. Add the sauce mix and bring it to a quick boil. Mix well.

6. Ladle the sauce over the salmon fillets. Serve immediately and get ready for the praise!

PREPARATION TIME: *Less than 5 minutes*
COOKING TIME: *5½ minutes*
SERVES: *4*

EACH SERVING: 212 Calories/ 74 Calories from Fat/ 35% Calories from Fat

Stir-Tossed Potato & Carrot Sticks

A colorful and tasty dish to cook when fresh leafy vegetables are not available. Potatoes and carrots, stir-tossed with a touch of garlic and oyster-flavored sauce, become irresistable. Fall back on this unique and easy dish when your pantry is running low.

3 medium potatoes
2 medium carrots
1 tablespoon oil
1 teaspoon minced garlic

SEASONING
1 teaspoon sugar
½ teaspoon salt
½ teaspoon cornstarch
2 cups chicken broth
2 tablespoons oyster-flavored sauce
1 tablespoon dry white wine
4 tablespoons diced scallions

1. Peel the potatoes and cut them into ½-inch slices. Stack 2 slices together and cut them into ¼-inch-wide strips no longer than 2 inches. Continue with the rest of the potato slices. Set them aside.

2. Peel the carrots and slice into strips about the same size as the potatoes. Set aside.

3. Mix the seasoning ingredients in a medium-sized bowl and set it aside.

4. Heat a wok on high for 30 seconds. Add the oil and swirl to coat the wok for 30 seconds longer. Add the garlic and stir-toss for 15 seconds. Add the seasoning mixture and bring it to a quick boil. Add the carrots and stir-toss for 1 minute. Add the potatoes, stir-toss, cover, and cook on medium heat for 10 minutes. Stir the vegetables occasionally to prevent sticking.

5. Spoon to a dish and serve hot.

PREPARATION TIME: *10-12 minutes*
COOKING TIME: *15 minutes*
SERVES: *4*

EACH SERVING: 194 Calories/ 35 Calories from Fat/ 17% Calories from Fat

White Rice

It is very easy to make boiled rice the Chinese way, from scratch. Master this technique and you will always enjoy fluffy rice. If you eat rice often, an electric rice cooker is a good investment. You are guaranteed a perfect pot of rice every time.

1 cup long grain white rice
1¾ cups cold water

1. Put the rice in a 1-quart saucepan and rinse it twice with cold water. Scoop off the excess water by cupping your hand over the rice grains. *Do not use a colander.* Add the cold water and bring the rice to a boil, uncovered, over high heat.

2. When the water bubbles to the top of the saucepan in about 7 minutes, turn the heat to medium and continue cooking uncovered. Stir with a fork or chopsticks occasionally to prevent sticking.

3. After about 5 minutes, when the water is almost evaporated, reduce the heat to simmer. Cover the saucepan with a tight-fitting lid and steam for about 20 minutes. Do not lift the lid during this time.

4. When the steaming is complete, fluff the rice once again with a fork or chopsticks. Replace the lid and let the rice stand until you are ready to serve.

PREPARATION TIME:	*2 minutes*
COOKING TIME:	*32 minutes*
YIELD:	*3½ cups cooked rice*
SERVES:	*7 (½ cup per serving)*
NOTE:	*Use the following formula to cook more rice: 2 cups of rice to 2¾ cups of water, yields 7 cups cooked rice; 3 cups of rice to 3¾ cups of water, yields about 10 cups of cooked rice. To succeed with these proportions, the rice must be rinsed twice and drained by cupping your hand over the rice grains. Use larger saucepans for larger quantities and allow for longer cooking time.*

EACH SERVING: 113 Calories/ 0 Calories from Fat/ 0% Calories from Fat

week 3

Roasted Pork Chops
Chinese Tossed Salad
Noodles in Broth
301 Calories/ 72 Calories from Fat/ 24% Calories from Fat

Roasted Pork Chops

My low-fat adaptation of the famed Cantonese roast pork, *char siu,* is every bit as tasty as the traditional dish. Longer marinating enhances the flavor of the pork. Overnight marinating is definitely preferable. Sliced cooked pork chops make a delicious topping on noodles and rice.

4 3-ounce pieces boneless pork chops, no more than ½-inch thick

MARINADE
¼ teaspoon 5-spice powder
¼ teaspoon black pepper
¼ teaspoon baking soda
2 tablespoons hoisin sauce
1 tablespoon chicken broth
2 tablespoons cold water
½ tablespoon lite soy sauce
1 tablespoon honey
1 tablespoon oyster-flavored sauce
1 tablespoon dry white wine
½ teaspoon minced garlic
1 tablespoon diced green scallions

1. Mix the marinade ingredients together until smooth in a large shallow dish with sides and set aside.

2. Wash the pork chops and pat them dry with paper towels. Trim the fat. Place the chops in the marinade dish and let them stand for 30 minutes or longer.

3. Preheat the oven to 425 degrees for 5 minutes. Place pork chops and marinade in a baking pan and roast for 10 minutes. Turn the chops over, baste them and roast for another 10 minutes.

4. Remove to a platter, top with the cooked marinade, and serve.

PREPARATION TIME: *5 minutes*
MARINATING TIME: *30 minutes or longer*
COOKING TIME: *20 minutes*
SERVES: *4*

EACH SERVING: 175 Calories/ 60 Calories from Fat/ 35% Calories from Fat

Chinese Tossed Salad

Combine your favorite lettuce (iceberg, romaine, bib, Boston) with bok choy and Napa cabbage, add straw mushrooms for elegance and pizazz and enjoy tossed green salad Chinese style.

¾ pound lettuce
¼ pound bok choy
¼ pound Napa cabbage
½ sweet red pepper
1 8-ounce can tiny peeled straw mushrooms, drained

1. Chill individual salad plates.

2. Rinse the greens and break them into bite-sized pieces or cut them on the bias into strips. Toss and mix the greens in a large bowl and then dish them out onto the chilled plates.

3. Trim the pepper and thin slice it into strips. Add several strips to each plate for color and flavor.

4. Top each serving with a tablespoon scoop of straw mushrooms and serve with a side bowl of Quick Sweet and Sour Dressing.

PREPARATION TIME:	*6 to 8 minutes*
COOKING TIME:	*None*
SERVES:	*8*
NOTE:	*The tiny peeled straw mushrooms are the most attractive. Ask your Chinese grocer for that special variety.*

EACH SERVING: 24 Calories/ 2 Calories from Fat/ 7% Calories from Fat

Quick Sweet & Sour Dressing

½ cup peach preserves
½ cup marmalade preserves
½ cup wine vinegar
¼ teaspoon salt
⅛ teaspoon pepper

Combine the above ingredients in a blender and whip for 30 seconds. This dressing can be made ahead and stored in the refrigerator for a least 2 weeks.

EACH SERVING: 40 Calories/ 0 Calories from Fat/ 0% Calories from Fat

Noodles in Broth

Whenever I need comfort on a cold winter night, this is the noodle dish I crave. Try it with spinach, bok choy, Napa cabbage or any of your favorite leafy greens. Please note that this is *not a soup to be served before meals,* but a noodle dish to be eaten *with your entree.*

¼ pound thin, dry noodles or vermicelli
8 cups cold water
10 ounces chopped spinach, fresh or frozen
4 cups chicken broth

1. Bring the water to a rolling boil in a 4-quart covered saucepan. Add the noodles and cook them uncovered for about 7 minutes – until they are tender to the bite.

2. While the noodles cook, bring the chicken broth to boil in a large, covered pot. Add the spinach and bring to a second boil. Remove from the heat, cover, and set aside.

3. When the noodles are done, drain and rinse them in cold water. Add them to the chicken broth pot, return the pot to the heat, and cook for 2 minutes.

4. Ladle to individual bowls and serve with the entree.

PREPARATION TIME: *Less than 5 minutes*
COOKING TIME: *24 minutes*
SERVES: *6*

EACH SERVING: 102 Calories/ 10 Calories from Fat/ 9% Calories from Fat

week 4

Braised Lamb with Leeks
Green Bean & Water Chestnut Salad
Fragrant Rice
392 Calories/ 77 Calories from Fat/ 20% Calories from Fat

Braised Lamb with Leeks

An easy and delicious way to cook lamb shanks – a favorite among the people of northern China. Leeks add the special dimension to this dish. Small lamb shanks weighing no more than ½ pound each are preferred. If these are not easy to find, 2 larger ones weighing a pound each will do. I usually like to cook this dish a day or two ahead, allowing the flavor to mellow.

4 8-ounce or 2 1-pound lamb shanks
1 whole leek
a 1-inch knob of gingerroot
½ tablespoon oil

MARINADE
2 tablespoons lite soy sauce
2 tablespoons whiskey

SEASONING
1 tablespoon sugar
¼ teaspoon black pepper
3 cups cold water
½ cup dry white wine
2 tablespoons oyster-flavored sauce
2 tablespoons cider vinegar

1. Mix the marinade ingredients in a large bowl, big enough for the shanks.

2. Rinse the shanks and pat them dry with paper towels. Add them to the marinade. Let stand for 30 minutes or longer, turning occasionally.

3. Trim the roots from the leek. Cut it in two where the white stem turns green. Cut the stem in two, lengthwise. Fan out the leaves and wash both the green and white parts carefully. (Dirt usually hides in the green stalk.) Cut each strip – greens and bulb – in half, lenghwise, once again. Finally, cut those strips into 1-inch pieces. Set aside.

4. Smash the gingerroot flat to release its full flavor. Set aside.

5. In a large bowl blend the sauce ingredients until smooth and set aside.

6. After the lamb has marinated for at least 30 minutes, heat a 6-quart saucepan for 30 seconds. Add the oil and swirl to coat the bottom of the saucepan for 30 seconds. Add the gingerroot and stir-toss for 10 seconds. Add the leeks. Stir-toss for about 1 minute. Add the lamb shanks *but reserve the marinade.* Brown both sides for about 1 minute a side. Add the marinade and seasoning and bring to a boil. Turn heat to low, cover, and let it simmer for 2 hours.

7. The meat will be so tender it will fall off the bones. Remove the bones, return the meat to the sauce, mix well, dish up and serve.

PREPARATION TIME:	*6-8 minutes*
MARINATING TIME:	*30 minutes*
COOKING TIME:	*2 hours and 6 minutes*
SERVES:	*6*
NOTE:	*This dish can be cooked several days ahead and reheated before serving.*

EACH SERVING: 210 Calories/ 53 Calories from Fat/ 26% Calories from Fat

Green Bean & Water Chestnut Salad

What could be more appealing than this salad when green beans are in season? Coupled with thinly-sliced, crunchy water chestnuts, this dish is also a treat for the eyes.

1 pound fresh green beans
1 cup water
1 11-ounce can sliced water chestnuts
1 teaspoon minced garlic

DRESSING
1 teaspoon sugar
½ teaspoon salt
⅛ teaspoon black pepper
1 tablespoon water
1 tablespoon lite soy sauce
1 tablespoon oyster-flavored sauce
½ tablespoon sesame seed oil

1. Mix the dressing ingredients in a small bowl and set aside.

2. Wash the green beans and snip off the ends. Place them in a large microwave-safe bowl, add the water, cover and microwave on high for 9 minutes. Drain and refresh the beans with cold water to stop the cooking. Pat them dry.

3. Add the dressing and stir thoroughly to coat the beans. Add the sliced water chestnuts and minced garlic. Toss again to blend well and serve.

PREPARATION TIME:	*8-10 minutes*

COOKING TIME: 9 minutes
SERVES: 4
MAKE AHEAD: Yes, serve chilled.

EACH SERVING: 83 Calories/ 16 Calories from Fat/ 19% Calories from Fat

Fragrant Rice

Using jasmine rice instead of regular long grain rice introduces a fragrance the Chinese call *Hsiang mi*, "fragrant rice." Our recipe sweetens the pot even more by adding celery, scallions and cilantro and using chicken broth instead of water.

1 cup jasmine rice
1 teaspoon oil
3 stalks of celery, diced (preferably stalks near the heart)
1½ cups chicken broth
2 tablespoons diced scallions
2 tablespoons minced cilantro or Chinese parsley
½ teaspoon freshly ground white pepper

1. Put the rice in a large bowl and rinse it twice in cold water. Pour off the excess water by cupping your hand over the rice grains. Do not use a colander. Set aside.

2. Heat a 2-quart saucepan, add the oil and swirl it for 15 seconds to coat the pan. Add the celery and stir-toss for 45 seconds. Add the chicken broth and bring it to a boil. Add the rice and bring the pot to a second boil. Boil until the broth bubbles to the top, about 3 minutes. Turn the heat to medium and continue cooking, uncovered. Stir occasionally to prevent sticking.

3. When the broth is mostly evaporated (after about 5 minutes) reduce the heat to simmer, cover the pot with a tight-fitting lid and steam for 20 minutes more. Do not lift the lid during this time.

4. When the steaming is complete, fluff the rice, mix in the scallions, cilantro and pepper, fluff again, and serve immediately.

PREPARATION TIME: 5 minutes
COOKING TIME: 31 minutes
SERVES: 8 (½ cup servings)

EACH SERVING: 99 Calories/ 8 Calories from Fat/ 9% Calories from Fat

Seasonal Celebrations: Four Fabulous Parties

Throwing a Chinese party need not intimidate you. While our parties are known for their many courses, elegant dishes and lavish presentations, we Chinese are also known for our ingenuity. *Chinese-Party-Made-Easy – is my goal.* You will find that our:

- Step-by-step party plan and
- Careful selection of dishes

make it both easy and enjoyable to throw a Chinese party.

The parties we have designed focus on a season of the year – Spring, Summer, Fall and Winter – and feature a unique Chinese method of food preparation and cooking – Mongolian Grill, Skewers, Wontons, and Firepots. The Chinese people are very sensitive to the seasons and their foods, flowers, flavors and moods. In this party collection, we have tried to capture the mood of each season and we feature those special foods abundant at that time of year.

Each person has their own approach to throwing a dinner party.

- Donna's approach is to have all the ingredients ready, but invite the guests to share in chopping, marinating, skewering, and cooking. This assumes the guests are easy-going and interested in learning something new about Chinese cooking.

- I, Liz, prefer a more formal – and better organized – approach. Meat and fish are chopped and marinated before guests arrive and dessert is readied. Guests join in skewering, wrapping wontons, grilling or using the firepots.

When you are cooking a number of dishes, the key to success is to be *very familiar with the recipes* and *have a clear, step-by-step, game plan* that melds the individual steps for the six different dishes into a single, manageable process. You'll find our game plan for each of the 4 parties we designed in Seasonal Celebrations on the page preceding the recipes.

I recommend you read and reread the party plan and the recipes before you begin to shop or prepare for your party. Then get ready to have a fabulous time as you join us in celebrating the seasons!

celebrating
SPRING

"The sky is whole and clear. The earth is whole and firm. The spirit is whole and strong. The valley is whole and full. The ten thousand things are whole and alive." • Tao Te Ching
• Time to gather friends, cook outdoors, and celebrate the return of fullness.

1 Shrimp on a Mongolian Grill

2 Beef on a Mongolian Grill

3 Cucumber Soup

4 Asparagus Spears

5 Noodles with Bean Sprouts & Scallions

6 A Taste of Spring

The Party Plan

☑ *Before you begin – read over each recipe in your party menu at least twice.*

☑ *2 hours before guests arrive do the individual steps listed in each recipe in the sequence shown below.*

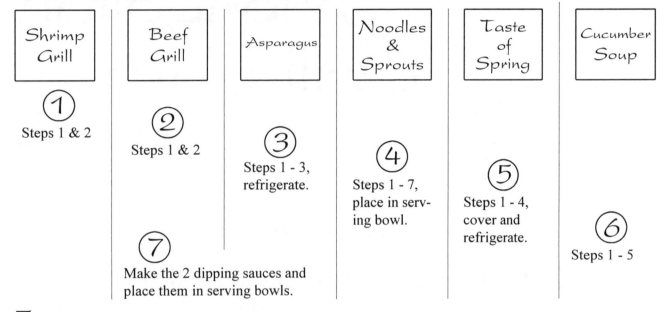

Shrimp Grill	Beef Grill	Asparagus	Noodles & Sprouts	Taste of Spring	Cucumber Soup

① Steps 1 & 2

② Steps 1 & 2

③ Steps 1 - 3, refrigerate.

④ Steps 1 - 7, place in serving bowl.

⑤ Steps 1 - 4, cover and refrigerate.

⑥ Steps 1 - 5

⑦ Make the 2 dipping sauces and place them in serving bowls.

☑ *After completing the above steps and ½ hour before your guests arrive, complete these preparations.*

⑧ Set the table – add the dipping sauces, asparagus spears and bowl of noodles.

⑨ Prepare the grill.

⑩ Grill the beef.

⑪ Grill the shrimp.

Enjoy! Bon Appetit!

⑫ Complete step #6 in cucumber soup instructions – ladle into individual soup bowls.

⑬ Take the fruit platter out of the refrigerator and set it on the table.

Spring Mongolian Grill Party

Shrimp on a Mongolian Grill
Beef on a Mongolian Grill
Cucumber Soup
Asparagus Spears
Noodles with Bean Sprouts & Scallions
A Taste of Spring
341 Calories/ 66 Calories from Fat/ 19% Calories from Fat

Shrimp on a Mongolian Grill

Mongolia was famous for its grilled beef and lamb. The Mongols used a special round metal grill called a "Mongolian grill." The modern version that I recommend is the Burton Super Stove Top Grill. It is easy to use and will bring the savory delight of ancient cooking into your modern kitchen. (See drawing on page 184.) Large prawns or shrimp can be cooked in minutes on this ingenious grill.

1 pound large shrimp in the shell, about 20

MARINADE
1 tablespoon cornstarch
1 teaspoon sugar
1 teaspoon salt
a dash of white pepper
1 tablespoon whiskey
1 tablespoon water

1. Shell the shrimp, leaving the tail on. Devein, rinse, drain and pat the shrimp dry with paper towels.

2. Mix the marinade ingredients in a large bowl until smooth. Add the shrimp and mix to coat well. Let them marinate for 30 minutes or longer.

3. Place the super top grill over the large burner on your stove. Fill the reservoir of the drip pan with approximately 2 cups of water. Refill it as needed, adding small amounts carefully.

4. When the shrimp has marinated for at least 30 minutes, preheat the grill on high for 2 minutes. Add the shrimp and grill for 2 minutes.

5. Serve with one or two dipping sauces. See below for recipes.

PREPARATION TIME:	*12 - 15 minutes*
MARINATING TIME:	*30 minutes*
COOKING TIME:	*6 minutes*
SERVES:	*8*
NOTE:	*The grill can also be used over a portable burner.*

EACH SERVING: 41 Calories/ 3 Calories from Fat/ 8% Calories from Fat

Honey Mustard Dipping Sauce

4 teaspoons Dijon mustard
2 tablespoons honey
¼ cup of cold water
2 tablespoons dry white wine
1 tablespoon Maggi seasoning
¼ teaspoon black pepper
2 teaspoons minced garlic

1. Combine the ingredients in a blender and whip for 30 seconds. This dip can be made ahead of time and stored in the refrigerator to at least 2 weeks.

EACH SERVING: 25 Calories/ 2 Calories from Fat/ 6% Calories from Fat

Hot & Spicy Dipping Sauce

½ tablespoon cornstarch
1½ teaspoons sugar
1 cup of cold water
2 tablespoons Hunan chili paste
2 tablespoons oyster-flavored sauce
2 tablespoons ketchup

1. Combine the cornstarch and cold water and mix until well-blended. Add the other ingredients and mix well. Place in a microwave-safe dish, cover, and cook on high for 2 minutes. Give the dish a quarter turn, cover, and cook for another 2 minutes.

2. The amount of Hunan chili paste you use determines how hot the sauce will be. For fiery hot sauce, use 2 to 3 tablespoons; for medium hot, 1 to 1½ tablespoons; for mild sauce, use ½ to 1 tablespoon. (Different brands of Hunan chili paste also vary in intensity. For best results, experiment before party time!)

EACH SERVING: 5 Calories/ 0 Calorie from Fat/ 4% Calories from Fat

Beef on a Mongolian Grill

The Mongols who conquered China in the 13th Century loved to grill their meat. The Burton Super Stove Top Grill (see drawing below) is very similar in shape and design to the Mongolian grill. It is teflon-coated and has a reservoir that holds water. Cooking beef this way is a healthy alternative to stir-frying. No oil is needed.

1 pound round steak, partially frozen

MARINADE
1 tablespoon cornstarch
1 teaspoon sugar
¼ teaspoon black pepper
2 tablespoons cold water
2 tablespoons oyster-flavored sauce
1 tablespoon dry white wine

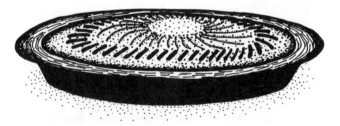

1. Trim the round steak, and cut it, with the grain, into 1½-inch strips. Then cut each strip into julienne slices.

2. In a large bowl, mix the marinade ingredients until smooth. Add the beef slices. Stir well, to evenly coat all the beef and let stand for 30 minutes or longer.

3. Place the grill over a large burner—either on an electric or gas stove. Fill the reservoir of the drip pan with approximately 2 cups of water and refill it as needed.

4. When the beef has marinated for at least 30 minutes, preheat the grill on high for 2 minutes. Divide the beef into two batches. Spread one batch evenly on the grill. Cook for 5 minutes. Remove the cooked beef and add the second batch. Serve hot.

PREPARATION TIME: 6 - 8 minutes
MARINATING TIME: 30 minutes
COOKING TIME: 12 minutes
SERVES: 8
NOTE: The grill can also be used over a portable burner.

EACH SERVING:89 Calories/ 23 Calories from Fat/ 25% Calories from Fat

Cucumber Soup

Light and refreshing, this soup adds an elegant touch to any party or meal.

1 small cucumber
1 small carrot
4 large mushrooms
4 cups chicken broth
2 egg whites, lightly beaten

GARNISH
1 tablespoon thinly-sliced scallions

1. In a 2-quart saucepan, bring the broth to a boil on high heat. While it is cooking, prepare the vegetables.

2. Clean and trim the carrot. Thin-slice it in rounds and set aside.

3. Wash and peel the cucumber, cutting off both ends. Quarter it lengthwise. Thin-slice each quarter, crosswise, and set aside.

4. Clean and thin-slice the mushrooms, cutting across the cap and stem. Set aside.

5. When the broth comes to a boil, add the carrot slices and turn the heat to medium.

6. Turn off the heat and drizzle in the egg whites. Add salt and pepper to taste and ladle the soup into individual bowls. Garnish with the sliced scallions and serve.

PREPARATION TIME: 8 - 10 minutes
COOKING TIME: 17 minutes
SERVES: 8

EACH SERVING: 29 Calories/ 6 Calories from Fat/ 20% Calories from Fat

Asparagus Spears

A quick and simple way to serve asparagus at its best. Pick firm and unblemished spears. Take advantage of the lower prices when asparagus is in season and serve this dish often.

1½ pounds fresh asparagus spears
¼ cup chicken broth
2 teaspoons minced garlic

DRESSING
1 teaspoon sugar
¼ teaspoon black pepper
2 tablespoons lite soy sauce
½ teaspoon sesame seed oil

1. Snap off and discard the tough end of each asparagus spear. (If you bend the stalk using both hands, they will usually break at the woody part of the stem.) Wash and drain the spears. Place them in a microwave-safe dish. Add the chicken broth and garlic.

2. Cover the dish and microwave on high for 3 minutes. Pour off the liquid. Mix the dressing ingredients in a small cup and add to the cooked asparagus. Blend carefully but well.

3. This dish is delicious hot or cold. To chill for serving, refrigerate for at least ½ hour.

PREPARATION TIME: *5 minutes*
COOKING TIME: *3 minutes*
CHILLING TIME: *30 minutes (optional)*
SERVES: *8*
MAKE AHEAD: *Yes, serve chilled.*

EACH SERVING: 23 Calories/ 7 Calories from Fat/ 26% Calories from Fat

Noodles with Bean Sprouts & Scallions

It's hard to believe that something so simple can taste so good! I have adapted a favorite noodle dish served in *dim sum* houses and made it low-fat and still yummy. For this recipe you need to buy the special "wonton" noodles – fresh, thin noodles made with a touch of eggs. The noodles cook very quickly and are best serve *al dente*. They also come in long strands that make an ideal birthday celebration. Long noodles symbolize long life!

2 3-ounce bundles of fresh thin Chinese wonton noodles

2 quarts + 1 quart warm water from the tap
1 small onion
¼ pound fresh bean sprouts
3 large scallions
2 teaspoons sesame seed oil

SEASONING FOR NOODLES
½ tablespoon sugar
¼ teaspoon salt
2 tablespoons cider vinegar
½ tablespoon sesame seed oil
1 tablespoon Maggi seasoning

SAUCE
1 teaspoon sugar
¼ teaspoon cornstarch
¾ cup chicken broth
1½ tablespoons oyster-flavored sauce
1 tablespoon dry white wine

1. Bring 2 quarts of warm water to a rolling boil in a 4-quart saucepan. Unfold each bundle of noodles and gently place it in the boiling water. Once the noodles begin to soften, unravel the strands, so they won't stick together. Cook, uncovered for about 2 minutes – until *al dente*. Rinse quickly in a colander under cold running water. Place the noodles on a large serving platter or bowl and cut into 4-inch lengths.

2. Mix the noodle seasoning in a small bowl and add it to the noodles. Blend well, using your hands, and set aside.

3. Bring a quart of warm water to a rolling boil. Turn off heat and add the bean sprouts. Let stand for about 2 minutes. Drain and refresh in cold water. Drain again and spread bean sprouts on top of the noodles. Set aside.

4. Wash and trim the scallions. Thin-slice them lengthwise, white and greens, into slivers.

5. Trim and peel the onion. Cut it in half, and slicing with the grain, cut each half into thin slivers. Set aside.

6. In a large bowl, combine and mix the sauce ingredients until smooth. Set aside.

7. Heat a wok on high for 30 seconds. Add 1½ tablespoons of sesame seed oil and swirl to coat the wok evenly for 30 seconds. Add the onion strips and scallion slivers. Stir-toss for 1 minute. Add the sauce and bring to a quick boil. Cook for 1 more minute. Ladle sauce over the bean sprouts and noodles, toss well and serve.

PREPARATION TIME: 8-10 minutes
SOAKING TIME: 2 minutes

COOKING TIME: 7 minutes
SERVES: 8

EACH SERVING: 107 Calories/ 21 Calories from Fat/ 20% Calories from Fat

A Taste of Spring

A creative way to show off Mother Nature's bounty. This desert—with its play of colors, shapes and tastes—brings an elegant meal to a delightful conclusion.

1 1-inch thick round slice of watermelon, about 2½ pounds
1 large kiwi
1 firm but ripe nectarine
16 fresh raspberries

1. Cut the watermelon round into 8 wedges and trim the rind. Arrange the wedges, top tips touching in the center, on a 12-inch platter.

2. Cut off the ends and peel the kiwi. Cut the fruit in quarters, then in eighths. Place them between the watermelon slices.

3. Peel the nectarine, cut it in half and gently remove the seeds. Cut each half in quarters, then thin-slice each quarter into 3 or 4 slices, lengthwise. Place 3 to 4 slices in a pinwheel pattern on top of each wedge of watermelon.

4. Gently rinse and drain the raspberries. Place 4 raspberries between the slices of nectarines.

5. Diners help themselves to a portion of the fruit medley.

PREPARATION TIME: 5 - 10 minutes
SERVES: 8

EACH SERVING: 52 Calories/ 6 Calories from Fat/ 10% Calories from Fat

celebrating
SUMMER

"Ten thousand flowers in Spring, the moon in Autumn, a cool breeze in Summer, snow in Winter. If your mind isn't clouded by unnecessary things, this is the best season of your life." • *Wu-Men* • Celebrate Summer with a skewers party. Everybody chops!

1 Shrimp on a Stick

2 Sichuan Beef on Skewers

3 Chicken on Skewers

4 Sweet Sugar Snap Peas

5 Rice with a Tropical Flair

6 Fruit on a Stick

The Party Plan

☑ *Before you begin – read over each recipe in your party menu at least twice.*

☑ *2 hours before guests arrive do the individual steps listed in each recipe in the sequence shown below.*

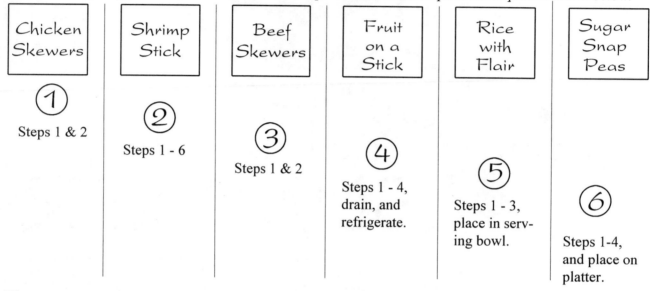

Chicken Skewers	Shrimp Stick	Beef Skewers	Fruit on a Stick	Rice with Flair	Sugar Snap Peas
①	②	③	④	⑤	⑥
Steps 1 & 2	Steps 1 - 6	Steps 1 & 2	Steps 1 - 4, drain, and refrigerate.	Steps 1 - 3, place in serving bowl.	Steps 1-4, and place on platter.

☑ *After completing the above steps and ½ hour before your guests arrive, complete these preparations.*

⑦ Soak 60 bamboo skewers – enough for shrimp, beef and chicken.

⑧ Prepare the grill.

⑨ Set the table – add the platter of peas and bowl of rice.

⑩ Set out the marinated shrimp, beef and chicken.

⑪ Drain the skewers and separate them into 3 batches.

⑫ Demonstrate how to skewer shrimp, beef and chicken.

⑬ Invite guests to skewer and grill their own combination of shrimp, beef and chicken.

⑭ Set out the fruit sticks.

Enjoy! Bon Appetit!

Sum mer
Skewers Party

Shrimp on a Stick
Sichuan Beef on Skewers
Chicken on Skewers
Sweet Sugar Snap Peas
Rice with a Tropical Flair
Fruit on a Stick
344 Calories/ 48 Calories from Fat/ 14% Calories from Fat

Shrimp on a Stick

Shrimp marinated in a mustard sauce and coated with Rice Krispies make a smashing dish. To preserve the shrimp meat texture, be sure to preheat the oven and broil the shrimp for no more than 5 minutes. Serve while still hot and crispy.

1 pound large shrimp in the shell, about 25 to 30
25 to 30 8-inch bamboo skewers
1¼ cups Rice Krispies
vegetable spray

MARINADE
1 teaspoon sugar
1 teaspoon salt
4 teaspoons Dijon mustard
4 teaspoons whiskey
4 teaspoons honey
1 tablespoon Maggi seasoning
1 tablespoon cold water
2 teaspoons grated onion
2 teaspoons grated gingerroot

1. Shell the shrimp, leaving the tail on. Devein, rinse, drain and pat the shrimp dry with paper towels. Slit open and fan out each shrimp. Place them in a large bowl.

2. Mix the marinade ingredients in a small bowl and pour over the shrimp. Stir the shrimp several times to ensure even coating. Let them marinate for 30 minutes or longer.

3. Soak the bamboo skewers in cold water for 30 minutes.

4. Place the *Rice Krispies* in the center of a 3-foot-long sheet of wax paper. Fold the sheet in two, lenghwise, and create an envelope to seal in the cereal. Crush the cereal with a rolling pin or round drinking glass. Set aside.

5. Prepare the outdoor grill or preheat the oven to broil for 5 minutes. If cooking indoors, line a large baking sheet with aluminum foil. Spray it with vegetable oil and set aside.

6. When the shrimp has marinated for at least 30 minutes, begin threading them on the skewers. Insert the skewer through the entire shrimp starting with the tail. Repeat until all are threaded. Roll the skewered shrimp, one skewer at a time, in the crushed cereal, evenly coating both sides.

7. Line up the skewers on a baking sheet for inside broiling or a platter to take outside to the grill. *Cook for only 5 minutes*. This prevents toughening and preserves the delicate texture. Serve immediately.

PREPARATION TIME:	*20 - 22 minutes*
MARINATING TIME:	*30 minutes*
COOKING TIME:	*5 minutes*
SERVES:	*8*
MAKE AHEAD:	*Yes. Marinate and skewer ahead of time. Then, just before serving, roll the shrimp in the crushed cereal and broil or grill.*
NOTES:	*Do not reheat this dish. The shrimp become tough.*
	When using smaller shrimp (about 40 to a pound), cut the cooking time to 4 minutes.
	Dry white wine can be substituted for the whiskey, but the dish is less tasty.

EACH SERVING: 76 Calories/ 6 Calories from Fat/ 9% Calories from Fat

Sichuan Beef on Skewers

This delicious dish is a perfect finger food for picnics, cocktail parties or any festive occasion. While these treats are expensive in Chinese restaurants, you can easilyand inexpensively make them at home. Tasty hot or cold, this dish is a great make-ahead appetizer.

¼ pound round steak, partially frozen
8 12-inch bamboo skewers

MARINADE
½ teaspoon cornstarch
¼ teaspoon sugar
¼ teaspoon baking soda
⅛ teaspoon black pepper
1 tablespoon lite soy sauce
½ tablespoon Hunan chili paste
½ tablespoon oyster-flavored sauce
1 tablespoon dry white wine
1 teaspoon sesame seed oil
1 teaspoon minced garlic

1. Soak the skewers in cold water for ½ hour. Set aside. In a medium-sized bowl, mix the marinade ingredients until smooth. Set aside.

2. Trim the fat from the flank steak. Slice the meat against the grain into ¼-inch wide strips, making 8 slices. Add these to the marinade mixture, turning the slices several times to coat them evenly. Marinate for 30 minutes or longer.

3. Prepare the outdoor grill or preheat the oven on broil for 5 minutes.

4. After the meat has marinated for at least 30 minutes, weave a skewer like a needle through the center of each slice of beef. Place the skewers side by side on a cookie sheet or platter (one with edges) and pour the remaining marinade over the beef slices. If cooking outside, place the skewers directly on the grill.

5. Cook about 4 inches from the heat for 6 minutes on each side. For rarer meat, broil or grill only 4 minutes on each side. For well-done meat, try 8 minutes a side.

PREPARATION TIME:	8 - 10 minutes
MARINATING TIME:	30 minutes or longer
COOKING TIME:	12 - 16 minutes
SERVES:	8
MAKE AHEAD:	Yes
VARIATION:	For a spicier dish, increase the Hunan chili paste to 1 tablespoon.
EACH SERVING:	26 Calories/ 6 Calories from Fat/ 23% Calories from Fat

Chicken on Skewers

This communal dish gets everyone involved in the preparation, cooking *and* eating! Ideal for Summer – or anytime you fancy chicken – this low-calorie and tasty dish can be served as an appetizer or entree. The whiskey in the marinade adds zip, but dry white wine is a good, while less tasty, substitute.

1 medium chicken breast, skinned, boned and partially frozen
24 to 28 8-inch bamboo skewers

MARINADE
1 teaspoon cornstarch
½ teaspoon sugar
½ teaspoon baking soda
⅛ teaspoon white pepper
1 tablespoon hoisin sauce
1 tablespoon ketchup
1 tablespoon oyster-flavored sauce
1 tablespoon whiskey
1 teaspoon grated gingerroot
1 teaspoon minced garlic

1. In a large bowl, mix the marinade ingredients until smooth. Set aside.

2. Trim the fat and cut the breast into very thin slices, about 3 inches long and 1 inch wide. You should get about 25 slices. Add the sliced chicken to the marinade. Mix well and let stand for 30 minutes or longer.

3. Prepare the outdoor grill or preheat the oven on broil for 5 minutes. If cooking indoors, line a cookies sheet (one that has edges) with aluminum foil.

4. After the chicken has marinated for at least 30 minutes, weave a skewer like a needle through the center of each slice of chicken. If slices are short, combine two or more on one skewer. Place the skewers side by side on the cookie sheet for inside broiling or on a platter to take outside to the grill. Mix the remaining marinade with ¼ cup of cold water and pour over the skewers.

5. Cook about 4 inches from the heat for 8 minutes on the first side and 7 minutes on the second. Serve hot.

PREPARATION TIME:	*25 - 30 minutes*
MARINATING TIME:	*30 minutes*
COOKING TIME:	*15 minutes*
SERVES:	*8*
EACH SERVING:	*52 Calories/ 8 Calories from Fat/ 15% Calories from Fat*

Sweet Sugar Snap Peas

Anytime you can find fresh sugar snap peas at your grocer's, snatch them up! When cooked this simple way, they delight any gourmand.

1 pound fresh sugar snap peas
2 50-cent-size slices gingerroot
½ tablespoon oil
½ teaspoon salt
½ cup chicken broth

1. With kitchen shears, snip the ends off the peapods. Rinse, drain and set aside.

2. Smash the gingerroot to release its full flavor. Set aside.

3. Heat a wok on high for 30 seconds. Add the oil and swirl to coat the wok for 30 seconds. Add the smashed gingerroot and stir-toss for 30 seconds. Add the salt and peapods. Stir-toss for 1 minute. Add the chicken broth, cover, and cook for 2½ minutes more.

4. Ladle to a bowl and serve.

PREPARATION TIME: *6-8 minutes*
COOKING TIME: *5 minutes*
SERVES: *8*
MAKE AHEAD: *Yes. Delicious hot or cold.*
NOTE: *Fresh sugar snap peas have a firm, tender skin. No stringing necessary.*

EACH SERVING: 33 Calories/ 9 Calories from Fat/ 27% Calories from Fat

Rice with a Tropical Flair

Bring Summer and sunshine into your meal with this tropical treat. Spiking the dish with vinegar gives it a sour bite that complements the sweet pineapple. I find this recipe a perfect way to use day-old rice. For a one-dish meal – simply add cooked chicken, steamed shrimp or leftover turkey.

2 cups day-old rice
4 egg whites, lightly beaten with 1 tablespoon Maggie seasoning
1 tablespoon oil
1 10-ounce can crushed pineapple in unsweetened juice, drained
1 tablespoon white vinegar

4 tablespoons diced scallions

1. Separate the rice clumps with your hands and set the rice aside.

2. Heat a wok on high for 1½ minutes. Add the oil and swirl to coat the work for 1½ minutes more until the wok is smoking. Pour in the egg white mixed with Maggie seasoning and stir quickly. Add the rice and stir-toss for 2 minutes. Add the pineapple. Stir-toss and mix for 1 minute. Add the vinegar and scallions and mix well with the rice. Turn the heat to medium, cover, and cook for 3 minutes.

3. Dish up the rice and serve hot.

PREPARATION TIME:	*Less than 5 minutes*
COOKING TIME:	*9 to 10 minutes*
SERVES:	*8*

EACH SERVING: 103 Calories/ 16 Calories from Fat/ 15% Calories from Fat

Fruit on a Stick

A simple yet delightful way to serve fresh fruit. Arrange the fruit-filled skewers in attractive designs on a large round platter or a rectangular tray. Add fresh flowers to create a festive flair. This dessert can be made ahead of time and refrigerated in a large covered container until serving time.

8 medium strawberries
½ medium cantaloupe
½ medium honeydew melon
8 8-inch bamboo skewers

1. Wash, hull and pat dry the strawberries. Set aside.

2. Scoop out and discard the cantaloupe's fiber and seeds. Cut it in half, then cut each half into thirds. Slip a sharp knife between the flesh and the rind and gently remove the flesh. Trim the narrow tips off both ends of each section and then cut the sections into 3 or more chunks. Set aside.

3. Prepare the honeydew melon as you did the cantaloupe.

4. Thread 4 or 6 melon chunks onto each skewer, alternating cantaloupe and honeydew chunks. Top each skewer with a fresh strawberry.

PREPARATION TIME:	*18 - 20 minutes*
SERVES:	*8*
MAKE AHEAD:	*Yes*

EACH SERVING: 54 Calories/ 3 Calories from Fat/ 4% Calories from Fat

celebrating FALL

"Coming, going, the waterbirds don't leave a trace, don't follow a path." • *Dogen* • Autumn is a time of passage. We treasure Summer's gifts, the brilliance of changing leaves and the hint of Winter in the air. Wrap up your memories and place your dreams in wontons as you chat with friends and celebrate the wonder of Autumn.

1 Turkey Wontons with Water Chestnuts & Cilantro

2 Vegetable Wontons

3 Steamed Shao Mais

4 Crunchy Peapods

5 Sichuan Noodles

6 Poached Pears with Raspberry Sauce

The Party Plan

☑ *Before you begin – read over each recipe in your party menu at least twice.*

☑ *2 hours before guests arrive do the individual steps listed in each recipe in the sequence shown below.*

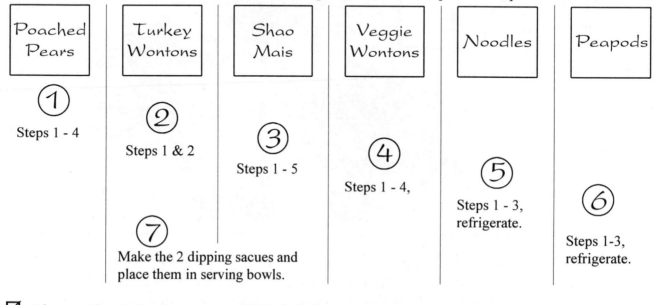

Poached Pears	Turkey Wontons	Shao Mais	Veggie Wontons	Noodles	Peapods

① Steps 1 - 4

② Steps 1 & 2

③ Steps 1 - 5

④ Steps 1 - 4,

⑤ Steps 1 - 3, refrigerate.

⑥ Steps 1-3, refrigerate.

⑦ Make the 2 dipping sacues and place them in serving bowls.

☑ *After completing the above steps and ½ hour before your guests arrive, complete these preparations.*

⑧ Set the table – add the dish of peapods, bowl of noodles and 2 bowls of dipping sauce.

⑨ Set out the marinated turkey, pork and vegetable fillings.

⑩ If your guests are to help wrap the wontons and shao mais, give each helper a cup of cold water and place the cookies sheets (covered with wax paper) in front of them.

⑪ Demonstrate wrapping wontons and folding shao mais.

⑫ Complete steps 5 - 6 in turkey wonton instructions; steps 7 - 8 in vegetable wonton instructions; steps 6 and 8 in shao mais instructions.

⑬ Cook the wontons and shao mais.

⑭ Set out the poached pears.

Enjoy!
Bon Appetit!

Fall Wonton Party

Turkey Wontons with Water Chestnuts & Cilantro
Vegetable Wontons
Steamed Shao Mais (Wontons)
Crunchy Peapods
Sichuan Noodles
Poached Pears with Raspberry Sauce

651 Calories/ 82 Calories from Fat/ 12% Calories from Fat

Turkey Wontons with Water Chestnuts & Cilantro

Wontons, literally translated as "swallowing clouds," are light and delicious. They come with a great variety of fillings. Here I have adapted the traditional fried wonton to make it meet low-fat yet gourmet standards. Once you've acquired the knack of wrapping wontons, you will want to enjoy them often. For this party, gather your guests to help you and teach them the art of wonton wrapping.

MARINADE
½ tablespoon cornstarch
1 teaspoon sugar
¼ teaspoon salt
⅛ teaspoon black pepper
1 tablespoon dry white wine
1 tablespoon Maggi seasoning
1 tablespoon cold water
1 teaspoon sesame seed oil

FILLING
6 ounces very lean ground turkey
½ cup fresh cilantro leaves, stalks trimmed and discarded
½ cup sliced water chestnuts
½ 14-ounce package of wonton wrappers
3 quarts + ½ cup cold water for each person wrapping wontons
2 cups chicken broth
1 10-ounce package frozen leaf spinach, thawed

1. In a large bowl, mix the marinade ingredients until smooth. Add the ground turkey and mix until well-blended. Let stand for 30 minutes or longer.

2. Rinse and drain the cilantro. Snap the leaves from the stalks and discard the stems.

3. Set out the cups of cold water for each person helping wrap wontons. Cover a couple of cookie sheets with wax paper so you'll have a place to collect the completed wontons.

4. After the turkey has marinated for at least 30 minutes, begin making the wontons. Take a wonton square in your hand. Place ¾ teaspoon of turkey filling in the center of the square. Top it with a cilantro leaf. Dip your fingers in the cup of cold water, moisten the edges of the wrapper and fold it into a triangle. Take the two ends, pinch them together and seal the connection with water. (See the diagram at the end of this recipe.) Place the wonton on one of the cookie sheets. Continue wrapping until you use up all the wrappers and filling. You should end up with about 27 to 30 wontons.

5. While you are wrapping the wontons, put the 3 quarts of water in a large saucepan, cover and bring it to a boil. If it boils before you are ready to cook the wontons, turn the heat to simmer.

6. In a separate saucepan, bring the chicken broth to a boil. Add the leaf spinach, cover, and cook on medium heat for 5 minutes. Turn off the heat and set it aside.

7. When you've wrapped a number of wontons and the water is boiling, drop about 15 wontons, one by one, into the boiling water. When the water returns to a boil, add 1 cup of cold water. When it comes to boil again, the wontons are ready. Use a Chinese wire mesh trainer or slotted spoon to ladle the wontons to a large soup serving bowl and set aside. Continue cooking the next batch and ladle them to the serving bowl.

8. When all the wontons are cooked, add the chicken broth-spinach mixture to the wontons and serve immediately. At the table, ladle individual servings into small bowls for each of the guests.

PREPARATION TIME:	*30 minutes (add a bit more time for your first effort!)*
MARINATING TIME:	*30 minutes*
COOKING TIME:	*15 to 20 minutes*
SERVES:	*8*

NOTE: A Chinese mesh strainer is an inexpensive and handy piece of equipment having many uses. In this case, it allows you to work quickly and efficiently strain the wontons before adding them to the chicken broth.

EACH SERVING: 151 Calories/ 25 Calories from Fat/ 16% Calories from Fat

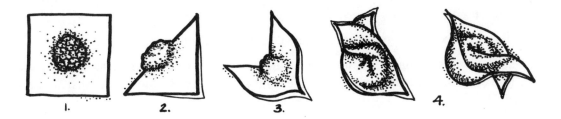

Vegetable Wontons

A recipe that both vegetarian and meat-eaters will love! Different from the more familiar wonton soup you will find in Chinese American restaurants, this soup is favored by the Chinese as a complete meal, late night snack, appetizer or a handy meal-in-one dish. At this party, guests will sample these yummy wontons and most likely ask you to make the dish again when they come to dine!

1 medium potato
1 small carrot
3 large scallions
½ 14-ounce package of wonton wrappers
½ pound of fresh peapods
2 cups cold water
3 quarts + ½ cup cold water for each person wrapping wontons
2 cups of chicken broth

SEASONING
1 teaspoon cornstarch
1 teaspoon sugar
1 teaspoon salt
¼ teaspoon black pepper
1 tablespoon Maggi seasoning
1 tablespoon water
½ tablespoon dry white wine

½ tablespoon sesame seed oil
1 teaspoon minced garlic

1. Put the potato and carrot in a saucepan and add enough cold water to cover. Cook on high until the water comes to a boil. Cover and turn the heat to medium. Continue to cook for about 15 minutes or until the vegetables are easily pierced with a fork. Drain the vegetables and cool under running water. Peel the potato and carrot and cut both vegetables into small pieces. Set aside.

2. In a small bowl, mix the seasoning ingredients until smooth. Set aside.

3. Clean and dice the scallions. Combine the scallions, potato and carrot in a food processor. Add the seasoning and fine-chop for 1 minute. Scrape the edges of the processor bowl to be sure that all the vegetables are evenly chopped.

4. With a pair of kitchen shears, cut off the top end of each peapod. Place the peapods in a large bowl and add 2 cups of cold water. Let them stand for 5 minutes to freshen and become crispy. Set aside.

5. Prepare cookie sheets covered in wax paper as a place to gather the wontons once you've wrapped them. Also pour cups of cold water for each person who will be wrapping wontons.

6. Begin making the wontons. Take a wonton square in your hand. Place ¾ teaspoon of vegetable filling in the center of the square. Dip your fingers in the cup of cold water, moisten the edges of the wrapper and fold it into a triangle. Take the two ends, pinch them together and seal the connection with water. (See the diagram immediately before this recipe.) Place the wonton on one of the cookie sheets. Continue wrapping until you use up all the wrappers and filling. You should end up with about 27 to 30 wontons.

7. While you are wrapping the wontons, put the 3 quarts of water in a large saucepan, cover and bring it to a boil. If it boils before you are ready to cook the wontons, turn the heat to simmer.

8. In a separate saucepan, bring the chicken broth to a boil. Add the peapods, cover, and cook on medium heat for 2 minutes. Turn off the heat and ladle the peapods into 8 separate soup bowls, distributing them evenly. Set them aside.

9. When you've wrapped a number of wontons and the water is boiling, drop about 15 wontons, one by one, into the boiling water. When the water returns to a boil, add 1 cup of cold water. When it comes to boil again, the wontons are ready. Use a Chinese wire mesh strainer or slotted spoon to ladle the wontons to each of the 8 individual soup bowls. Continue cooking the next batch and ladle them to the soup bowls.

10. When all the wontons are cooked, add the chicken broth to the soup bowls and serve immediately.

PREPARATION TIME:	*12 to 15 minutes*
COOKING TIME:	*41 minutes*
SERVES:	*8*

VARIATION:
NOTE:

VARIATION: *The wontons can be served as an appetizer without soup. When you do this add one or two dipping sauces. See the index; there are 5 different dipping sauces in A Wok A Week.*

NOTE: *A Chinese mesh strainer is an inexpensive and handy piece of equipment having many uses. In this case, it allows you to work quickly and efficiently strain the wontons before adding them to the chicken broth.*

EACH SERVING: 145 Calories/ 14 Calories from Fat/ 10% Calories from Fat

Steamed Shao Mais (Wontons)

Mandarin speakers called steamed wontons "shao mais." Steaming, rather than boiling, produces a neater and shaplier wonton. Shao mails look more like petals of a flower. Delightful to look at and even better to eat!

1 large scallion, with the greens
2 large garlic cloves
4 ounces of very lean ground pork
4 ounces fresh shrimp
1 8-ounce can of mushroom pieces and stems, drained
¾ pound of round wonton wrappers
nonfat vegetable spray

SEASONING FOR PORK
1 tablespoon cornstarch
1 teaspoon sugar
½ teaspoon salt
⅛ teaspoon black pepper
1 tablespoon cold water
1 tablespoon oyster-flavored sauce
1 tablespoon dry white wine

SEASONING FOR SHRIMP
1 teaspoon cornstarch
1 teaspoon sugar
¼ teaspoon salt
⅛ teaspoon white pepper
½ teaspoon dry white wine
1 teaspoon sesame seed oil

1. Trim the scallion and cut it into small pieces. Set aside. Skin the garlic cloves and put them, the scallion and the mushroom pieces in a food processor. Fine-chop for 1 minute. Set aside.

2. In a large bowl, mix the pork seasoning ingredients until smooth. Add the ground pork and blend well. Let stand for at least 15 minutes.

3. If the shrimp are not already shelled, do so. Devein them if necessary. Rinse well and pat them dry with a paper towel. Chop them into ½-inch sized pieces and set aside. In a medium-sized bowl, mix the shrimp seasoning ingredients until smooth. Add the shrimp pieces. Blend well. Let stand for at least 15 minutes.

4. While the pork and shrimp are marinating, put on a large pot of water to boil. When it boils, turn the heat to simmer and keep it ready to use in your steamer.

5. When the pork and shrimp have marinated for at least 15 minutes, mix them together in a large bowl. Add the chopped scallions-garlic-mushroom mixture. Blend well.

6. Fill the lower part of the steamer to the halfway mark with boiling water. Cover and bring it to a rolling boil. If the shao mais are not ready, turn the heat to simmer.

7. To make the shao mais, take a wonton round in your hand and wet the outer rim all around the edge. Place about ¾ teaspoon of filling in the center of the wrapper. Gather the sides of the wrapper around the filling, letting the wrapper pleat naturally. Press the gathered top together gently to be sure that it is sticking together and will cover the filling. Tap the shao mais bottom against a hard surface to make a flat bottom that will allow it to stand upright. (See diagram below.)

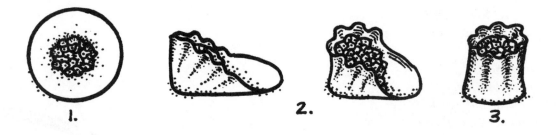

8. Continue wrapping shao mais until all wrappers and filling are used. Spray two heatproof platters that fit into your steamer with a coat of vegetable spray. Place the shao mais on the plate and the plate on a steamer rack. Put the rack in the steamer, cover and steam on high for 10 minutes. Remove and steam the second plate of shao mais in the same way.

9. Since these shao mais are well-seasoned, they can be served just as they are. However, if you prefer a dipping sauce, we recommend the two listed at the end of this recipe.

PREPARATION TIME: 28 to 30 minutes
MARINATING TIME: 15 minutes
COOKING TIME: 10 minutes for each plate of shao mais
SERVES: 8
NOTE: *If you cannot find round wonton wrappers, use a round cookie cutter to reshape square wrappers, or trim them by hand. Different brands of wonton wrappers vary in thickness. On the average you should get 60 to 65 sheets to a pound of wrappers. If you have leftover wrappers, put them in tightly-sealed plastic wrap and store them in a plastic bat in the freezer. Defrost before using.*

EACH SERVING: 191 Calories/ 22 Calories from Fat/ 11% Calories from Fat

Hoisin Dipping Sauce

½ cup Hoisin sauce
¼ cup chicken broth
½ tablespoon wine vinegar
½ tablespoon sesame seed oil
⅛ teaspoon black pepper

Combine the ingredients in a blender and whip for 30 seconds. This dip can be made ahead and stored in the refrigerator for at least two weeks.

EACH SERVING: 19 Calories/ 8 Calories from Fat/ 40% Calories from Fat

Hot & Spicy Dipping Sauce

½ tablespoon cornstarch
1½ teaspoons sugar
1 cup of cold water
2 tablespoons Hunan chili paste
2 tablespoons oyster-flavored sauce
2 tablespoons ketchup

1. Combine the cornstarch and cold water and mix until well-blended. Add the other ingredients and mix well. Place in a microwave-safe dish, cover, and cook on high for 2 minutes. Give the dish a quarter turn, cover, and cook for another 2 minutes.

2. The amount of Hunan chili paste you use determines how hot the sauce will be. For fiery hot sauce, use 2 to 3 tablespoons; for medium hot, 1 to 1½ tablespoons; for mild sauce, use ½ to 1 tablespoon. (Different brands of Hunan chili paste also vary in intensity. For best results, experiment before party time!)

EACH SERVING: 5 Calories/ 0 Calorie from Fat/ 4% Calories from Fat

Crunchy Peapods

The delicate flavor and wonderful crunch of Chinese peapods are enhanced by this delicious dressing. Freshness is paramount: pick firm and unblemished pods and serve this recipe chilled.

1 pound fresh Chinese peapods
1 cup water

DRESSING
1½ teaspoons sugar
½ teaspoon salt
⅛ teaspoon black pepper
1 tablespoon lite soy sauce
½ tablespoon sesame seed oil
1 teaspoon minced garlic

1. Mix the dressing ingredients in a small bowl and set aside.

2. Wash and snip off the top of each peapod. Place the peapods in a large microwave-safe dish and add the cup of water. Cover and microwave on high for 2½ minutes. Drain the peapods and refresh them in cold water to stop the cooking. Pat them dry.

3. Pour the dressing over the peapods and toss to mix well. Serve immediately or chill and serve.

PREPARATION TIME:	*8 -10 minutes*
COOKING TIME:	*2½ minutes*
CHILLING TIME:	*30 minutes*
SERVES	*8*
MAKE AHEAD:	*Yes*

EACH SERVING: 35 Calories/ 8 Calories from Fat/ 23% Calories from Fat

Sichuan Noodles

This savory noodle dish is a specialty of Sichuan province. Ideal for lunch, brunch, or dinner, these noodles are a wonderful complement to any entree. Sichuan noodles are delicious hot or cold.

8 cups (2 quarts) cold water
¼ pound thin dry noodles or vermicelli

DRESSING
1 teaspoon sugar
¼ teaspoon black pepper
1 tablespoon Hunan chili paste
½ tablespoon oyster-flavored sauce
½ tablespoon sesame seed oil
½ tablespoon lite soy sauce
½ tablespoon wine vinegar
2 tablespoons diced scallions
1 teaspoon minced garlic

1. Bring 2 quarts of water to a rolling boil in a 4-quart saucepan. Add the noodles and cook, uncovered, for about 7 minutes – until they are tender to the bite.

2. While the noodles are cooking, combine the dressing ingredients and blend them well.

3. Drain and rinse the noodles in a colander with cold running water. Transfer them to a large bowl. Pour the dressing mixture over the noodles. Mix well and serve hot or cold.

PREPARATION TIME:	*2 minutes*
COOKING TIME:	*12 to 15 minutes*
YIELD:	*3 cups cooked noodles*
SERVES:	*8*

EACH SERVING CONTAINS: 68 Calories/ 10 Calories from Fat/ 14% Calories from Fat

Poached Pears with Raspberry Sauce

An elegant and scrumptious dessert that can rival the sweet fare of any New York, Chicago, Atlanta or San Francisco restaurant. Serve this to top off your Wonton Party!

4 ripe Bosc pears
2 cups water
1 cup dry red wine
1 tablespoon grated gingerroot
1 lemon
½ cup + 1 tablespoon sugar
1 pint fresh or frozen raspberries

1. Peel the pears with a sharp paring knife. Start at the bottom and smoothly proceed to the top in a circular pattern. Try to keep the pear surface smooth and even, retaining the natural shape of the fruit.

2. Halve the pears, taking care to keep the stem connected to one side. Use a small spoon to scoop out the core and seeds. Set the pears aside.

3. In a 3-quart, non-metalic, heatproof dish, add the 2 cups of water, red wine, ½ cup of sugar, and grated gingerroot. Rinse and peel the rind from the lemon. Cut the peel into strips and add them to mixture. Bring it to a rolling boil in about 6 minutes. Turn the heat to medium, gently lower the pears into the liquid and poach them for 20 minutes. Keep the dish partly covered as the pears poach. When a toothpick easily pierces the pears, they are done. Carefully remove the pear halves with a slotted spoon and place them in a container to cool. When the syrup has cooled, pour it over the pears and store them, covered, in the refrigerator for at least 2 hours.

4. While the pears are gaining flavor in the fridge, put the raspberries and one tablespoon of sugar in a blender and blend for 30 seconds to a minute. Set the sauce aside until serving time. When ready to serve the pears, make several 1½-inch-long incisions lengthwise in the wide section of the back of each pear half – from the base to the center of the fruit. Fan out the pear like a pleated shirt. Add 2 tablespoons of soaking liquid over the pear half. Top with a tablespoon or more of raspberry puree and serve with pride!

PREPARATION TIME:	*15 minutes*
COOKING TIME:	*26 minutes*
SERVES:	*8*
MAKE AHEAD:	*A must!*
NOTE:	*This recipe works well for a party of four, also. Give each guest a whole pear, being sure to match a half with a stem with its "stemless partner."*

EACH SERVING: 61 Calories/ 3 Calories from Fat/ 5% Calories from Fat

celebrating WINTER

"The soil is bare now, nor can foot feel, being shod. And for all this, nature is never spent; There lives the dearest freshness deep down things. . ." • *GM Hopkins* • Celebrate this hidden freshness around Chinese firepots. Friends come early and help cook.

1 Seafood Firepot

2 Vegetarian Firepot

3 Chicken Fingers

4 Sichuan Noodles

5 Fragrant Rice

6 Banana Flambe

The Party Plan

☑ *Before you begin – read over each recipe in your party menu at least twice.*

☑ *2 hours before guests arrive do the individual steps listed in each recipe in the sequence shown below.*

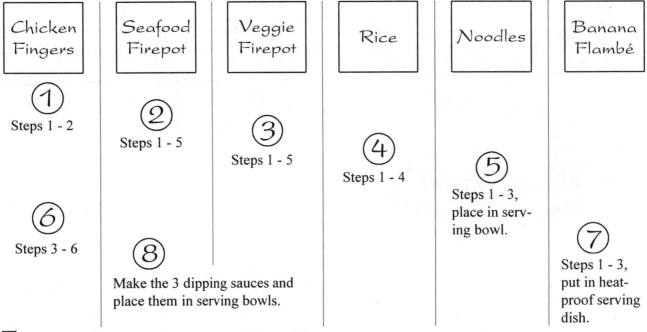

Chicken Fingers	Seafood Firepot	Veggie Firepot	Rice	Noodles	Banana Flambé
① Steps 1 - 2	② Steps 1 - 5	③ Steps 1 - 5	④ Steps 1 - 4	⑤ Steps 1 - 3, place in serving bowl.	⑦ Steps 1 - 3, put in heat-proof serving dish.
⑥ Steps 3 - 6	⑧ Make the 3 dipping sauces and place them in serving bowls.				

☑ *After completing the above steps and ½ hour before your guests arrive, complete these preparations.*

⑨ Set out the firepots (electric woks or frying pans) and cook the broth; reduce to simmer.

⑩ Set the table – place the platter of chicken fingers, and bowls of rice and noodles on the table.

⑪ Set out the platter of marinated seafood and the tray of vegetables.

⑫ Give each guest a wire mesh basket and 3 small bowls for dipping sauces.

⑬ Demonstrate firepot cooking.

⑭ At dessert time – step # 4 of banana flambé instructions

Enjoy!
Bon Appetit!

Win ter Firepot Party

Seafood Firepot

The traditional firepot is an unusual piece of equipment. (See the brush painting on page 209.) This covered pot with a center chimney has heated coals in the bottom section to cook the food. Electric woks or frying pans – because they maintain a consistent heat, are good modern substitutes. This seafood firepot dish is characterized by a medley of different tastes and flavors. The chef's task is to have the vegetables and seafood ready so the guests can cook their own meal.

1 pound fresh watercress
½ pound fresh bean sprouts
6 medium mushrooms
1 2-ounce package of glassy noodles
2 cups of hot water
8 large fresh shrimp, shelled
6 ounces fresh sea scallops
6 ounces crab (fresh or imitation)

1 2-ounce can of baby clams, drained
8 cups of clam juice, canned or bottled
2 cups cold water

SEAFOOD DIPPING SAUCE
¼ cup wine vinegar
½ cup cold water
1½ tablespoons Maggi seasoning or lite soy sauce
½ to 1 tablespoon Hunan chili paste (optional)

1. Wash and rinse the watercress twice to clean it thoroughly. Divide it in half, drain and set the bunches aside. Rinse the bean sprouts, drain and set them aside. Clean the mushrooms, trim the stems to ½ inch from the cap and thin-slice the mushrooms through caps and stems. Set aside.

2. Arrange half the watercress, and all the bean sprouts and mushrooms attractively on a large tray and set aside.

3. Soak the glassy noodles in 2 cups of hot water for 5 minutes. Drain and cut them into 2-inch lengths. Set aside.

4. Wash and pat dry the shrimp. Devein and split each shrimp in two, lengthwise. Arrange the shrimp attractively on a large platter, leaving room for the scallops, crab, clams and glassy noodles.

5. Wash and pat dry the scallops. Thin-slice them on the round. Add them to the platter with the shrimp. Separate the crab into smaller pieces and add it to the platter. Add the baby clams to the arrangement. Finally, add the glassy noodles and set the platter aside. Chill in the refrigerator, if there is some time before dinner.

6. Combine the ingredients for the dipping sauce, mix well, and divide it into 8 small bowls.

7. In a large pot, bring the clam juice and 2 cups of cold water to a boil. Transfer the broth to a large electric wok or frying pan big enough to serve as the firepot. About 5 minutes before serving, put half the watercress in the broth to cook.

8. Give each diner a wire mesh basket and a bowl of dipping sauce. Demonstrate how to use the firepot: place seafood and vegetables in the basket and immerse them in the hot broth to cook. When the food is cooked, place it on the diner's plate, ready to dip in sauce and enjoy. After the diners have eaten the seafood and vegetables, the cooking broth can be served as a soup or added to the rice.

PREPARATION TIME:	15 to 18 minutes
COOKING TIME:	8 minutes (for the broth)
SERVES:	8
NOTE:	Chicken broth can be substituted for the clam juice, but the flavor is not quite as rich.

EQUIPMENT: *It adds to the ambiance of the party if you can supply your guests with Chinese
wire mesh baskets, porcelain spoons and chopsticks – otherwise, use soup
ladles or slotted spoons – preferable ones with long handles.*

EACH SERVING: 140 Calories/ 9 Calories from Fat/ 7% Calories from Fat

Vegetarian Firepot

The firepot is probably the mother of Swiss fondue. Here is a firepot that vegetable lovers can indulge in to their heart's content. Four kinds of vegetables, tofu, glassy noodles and egg whites make up this scrumptious high-fiber meal. If you are a strict vegetarian, substitute vegetable broth for the chicken broth.

¼ pound fresh peapods
1 pound bok choy
1 15-ounce can straw mushrooms, drained
1 cup of sliced water chestnuts, drained
1 10.5-ounce package Mori-nu firm tofu
1 2-ounce package glassy noodles
2 cups hot water
4 egg whites, slightly beaten
8 cups chicken broth

1. Trim the stem ends of the peapods and soak them for 5 minutes in enough cold water to cover. Drain and set aside.

2. Wash the bok choy, cut off the end of the stem and separate the leaves. Thin-slice it on the bias into ½-inch-wide pieces.

3. Arrange the bok choy, peapods, water chestnuts and straw mushrooms attractively on a tray, leaving room for the glassy noodles and tofu.

4. Soak the glassy noodles in hot water for 5 minutes. Drain and cut them into 2-inch lengths. Add them to the vegetable tray along with the straw mushrooms.

5. Drain the tofu and cut it into 1-inch squares about ¼-inch thick. Add it to the vegetable tray. Place the egg whites in a small serving bowl. You are now ready for the firepot!

6. Combine the ingredients for the dipping sauce, mix well, and divide into 8 small bowls.

7. In a large pot, bring the broth to a boil. Transfer it to an electric wok or frying pan large enough to hold both the broth and the vegetables.

8. Give each guest a wire mesh basket, a bowl of dipping sauce, and an individual dinner bowl. Diners cook their own food by placing vegetables and tofu in the hot broth. Since bok choy takes longer to cook, you might wish to cook enough for a first serving before diners begin to cook for themselves.

9. Demonstrate how to use the firepot. First place a spoonful of egg whites in one of the diner's bowl and cover it with the boiling broth. Then place the vegetables and tofu in a mesh basket and immerse them in the hot broth to cook. When the food is cooked, place it in the diner's bowl, ready to dip in sauce and enjoy. After eating the vegetables, dish up the cooking broth to enjoy with rice.

PREPARATION TIME:	*12 to 15 minutes*
COOKING TIME:	*8 minutes (for the broth)*
SERVES:	*8*
NOTES:	*Vegetable broth can be substituted for the chicken broth, if your diners are strict vegetarians.*
VARIATION:	*Fresh watercress, lettuce, zucchini, green beans, carrots and other leafy or root vegetables are delicious in this firepot.*
EQUIPMENT:	*It adds to the ambiance of the party if you can supply your guests with Chinese wire mesh baskets, porcelain spoons and chopsticks.*

EACH SERVING: 124 Calories/ 21 Calories from Fat/ 16% Calories from Fat

Honey Mustard Dipping Sauce
4 teaspoons Dijon mustard
2 tablespoons honey
¼ cup of cold water
2 tablespoons dry white wine
1 tablespoon Maggi seasoning
¼ teaspoon black pepper
2 teaspoons minced garlic

1. Combine the ingredients in a blender and whip for 30 seconds. This dip can be made ahead of time and stored in the refrigerator to at least 2 weeks.

EACH SERVING: 25 Calories/ 2 Calories from Fat/ 6% Calories from Fat

Hot & Spicy Dipping Sauce
½ tablespoon cornstarch
1½ teaspoons sugar
1 cup of cold water
2 tablespoons Hunan chili paste

2 tablespoons oyster-flavored sauce
2 tablespoons ketchup

1. Combine the cornstarch and cold water and mix until well-blended. Add the other ingredients and mix well. Place in a microwave-safe dish, cover, and cook on high for 2 minutes. Give the dish a quarter turn, cover, and cook for another 2 minutes.

2. The amount of Hunan chili paste you use determines how hot the sauce will be. For fiery hot sauce, use 2 to 3 tablespoons; for medium hot, 1 to 1½ tablespoons; for mild sauce, use ½ to 1 tablespoon. (Different brands of Hunan chili paste also vary in intensity. For best results, experiment before party time!)

EACH SERVING: 5 Calories/ 0 Calories from Fat/ 4% Calories from Fat

Chicken Fingers

You can quickly prepare this all-time favorite right in your own kitchen – even when your pantry is skimpy. Chicken fingers make a great entree and a delicious appetizer.

1 8-ounce chicken breast
1 egg white
2 tablespoons toasted sesame seeds
vegetable oil spray

MARINADE
2 teaspoons cornstarch
½ teaspoon sugar
¼ teaspoon salt
¼ teaspoon baking soda
¼ teaspoon white pepper
1 tablespoon dry white wine
½ teaspoon oyster-flavored sauce

1. Mix the marinade ingredients in a medium-sized bowl and set aside.

2. Remove all skin and fat from the chicken breast. Cut it into strips, 2 inches long and ¼ inch wide, making about 26 strips. Place the strips in the marinade bowl. Marinate them for 30 minutes or longer.

3. Lightly spray the surface of a baking sheet with vegetable oil. Preheat the oven to 375 degrees.

4. Beat the egg white in a chilled metal bowl until frothy. Add the sesame seeds and set aside.

5. After the chicken has marinated for at least 30 minutes, add the egg white and sesame seed mixture. Stir

well to coat the strips. Place the strips side by side on the baking sheet. Bake the strips for 5 minutes. Turn them over and continue baking for another 3 minutes.

6. Cool the Chicken Fingers for 5 minutes before removing them to a serving platter.

PREPARATION TIME:	*8-10 minutes*
MARINATING TIME:	*30 minutes*
COOKING TIME:	*8 minutes*
COOLING TIME:	*5 minutes*
SERVES:	*8*
NOTE:	*To make toasted sesame seeds, place raw seeds on a cookie sheet and bake in at 250-degrees for 30 minutes. Store leftover toasted seeds in an airtight jar.*

EACH SERVING: 50 Calories/ 12 Calories from Fat/ 24% Calories from Fat

Sichuan Noodles

This savory noodle dish is a specialty of Sichuan province. Ideal for lunch, brunch, or dinner, these noodles are a wonderful complement to any entree. To make a one-dish meal, simply add cooked chicken or turkey and some vegetables. Sichuan noodles are delicious hot or cold.

8 cups (2 quarts) cold water
¼ pound thin dry noodles or vermicelli

DRESSING
1 teaspoon sugar
¼ teaspoon black pepper
1 tablespoon Hunan chili paste
½ tablespoon oyster-flavored sauce
½ tablespoon sesame seed oil
½ tablespoon lite soy sauce
½ tablespoon wine vinegar
2 tablespoons diced scallions
1 teaspoon minced garlic

1. Bring 2 quarts of water to a rolling boil in a 4-quart saucepan. Add the noodles and cook, uncovered, for about 7 minutes – until they are tender to the bite.

2. While the noodles are cooking, combine the dressing ingredients and blend them well.

3. Drain and rinse the noodles in a colander with cold running water. Transfer them to a large bowl. Pour the dressing mixture over the noodles. Mix well and serve hot or cold.

PREPARATION TIME: 2 minutes
COOKING TIME: 12-15 minutes
YIELD: 3 cups cooked noodles
SERVES: 8

EACH SERVING : 68 Calories/ 10 Calories from Fat/ 14% Calories from Fat

Fragrant Rice

Using jasmine rice instead of regular long grain rice introduces a fragrance the Chinese call *Hsiang mi,* "fragrant rice." Our recipe sweetens the pot even more by adding celery, scallions and cilantro and using chicken broth instead of water.

1 cup jasmine rice
1 teaspoon oil
3 stalks of celery, diced (preferably stalks near the heart)
1½ cups chicken broth
2 tablespoons diced scallions
2 tablespoons minced cilantro or Chinese parsley
½ teaspoon freshly ground white pepper

1. Put the rice in a large bowl and rinse it twice in cold water. Pour off the excess water by cupping your hand over the rice grains. Do not use a colander. Set aside.

2. Heat a 2-quart saucepan, add the oil and swirl it for 15 seconds to coat the pan. Add the celery and stir-toss for 45 seconds. Add the chicken broth and bring it to a boil. Add the rice and bring the pot to a second boil. Boil until the broth bubbles to the top, about 3 minutes. Turn the heat to medium and continue cooking, uncovered. Stir occasionally to prevent sticking.

3. When the broth is mostly evaporated (after about 5 minutes) reduce the heat to simmer, cover the pot with a tight-fitting lid and steam for 20 minutes more. Do not lift the lid during this time.

4. When the steaming is complete, fluff the rice, mix in the scallions, cilantro and pepper, fluff again, and serve immediately.

PREPARATION TIME: 5 minutes
COOKING TIME: 31 minutes
SERVES: 8

EACH SERVING: 99 Calories/ 8 Calories from Fat/ 9% Calories from Fat

Banana Flambé

A low-fat version of the New Orleans all-time favorite. Who would guess that this sophisticated and elegant dessert is both easy to make and low in calories? Serve it as a perfect ending to any dinner or party.

4 medium-sized bananas
½ cup water
2 tablespoons + 2 tablespoons sugar
4 1½-inch wide strips of lemon peel
3 tablespoons brandy

SAUCE
1 cup fresh stawberries, sliced
1 tablespoon sugar

1. In a blender, puree the strawberries with 1 tablespoon sugar for 30 seconds. Set aside.

2. Peel the bananas and cut them into quarters. Set aside.

3. In a small non-metal pan, bring the water, 2 tablespoons sugar, and lemon peel to boil on high heat, stirring frequently. When the sugar water boils, in about 2 minutes, add the banana sections and cook for 3 minutes – or until they are soft and heated through.

4. Add the brandy to the bananas and light the sauce. When the flame has died, prepare individual servings of two banana sections each and top them with strawberry puree and serve immediately.

PREPARATION TIME:	*5 minutes*
COOKING TIME:	*6 minutes*
SERVES:	*8*
MAKE AHEAD:	*Yes. Refrigerate and serve cold later. Delicious hot or cold.*

EACH SERVING: 94 Calories/ 3 Calories from Fat/ 3% Calories from Fat

The Authors Introduce Each Other

Elizabeth Chiu King, born in Shanghai, is a woman of amazing energy and talent. I, Donna, first met Liz seven years ago at a journaling workshop in California. She gave me a copy of her delightfully practical book, *THE 15-MINUTE CHINESE GOURMET* (Macmillan, 1986) and I introduced her to the weight management manual I developed for Kaiser Permanente. We decided that week to collaborate on a new cookbook.

For Liz, cooking and sharing delicious food is an integral part of every social gathering. Her table is always a work of art; each dish, a rare treat for the palate. But perhaps the greatest marvel is the ease and elegance of her culinary talent. Whether she is preparing one of her 15-minute gourmet dishes for her family or an 18-course banquet for 43, she makes food preparation simple and splendid.

Liz is fluent in four Chinese dialects. She frequently returns to China to visit friends and relatives. Liz has been very active in spreading a love for and knowledge of Chinese cooking and culture since she came to America 27 years ago.

For me, an average American cook from the Midwest, Liz opens up a whole new world of appreciation of the colors, textures, delicate mix of tastes, smells, and elegant arrangements of food. She loves to cook. She loves to eat. *And she loves to make the ancient art of Chinese cooking something even the most average of cooks can learn with delight and master with confidence.*

Liz and her husband, Albert, live in Bloomfield Hills, Michigan.

Donna Dean has added new spice to my working on a cookbook. She writes with humor and clarity – and she has introduced me, Liz, to the world of 30% or less fat in cooking and eating.

Donna, a learning specialist, graphic designer and public health educator has extensive experience in the field of low-fat nutrition. She wrote the narrative for *HEALTH COUNTS, A FAT AND CALORIE GUIDE* (John Wiley and Son, 1991,) for Kaiser Permanente NorthWest Region, and developed all the participant materials that Kaiser Permanente uses in their nationally-marketed weight management program, *FREEDOM FROM FAT.*

Donna has a master's degree in Public Health Education from the University of Hawaii, School of Public Health. She has worked as a health educator and materials development specialist on local, regional, state, and national levels. Her publications are as varied as her talents: she has written *THE ANNUAL DIRECTOR'S REPORT TO CONGRESS* for the National Heart, Lung and Blood Institute in Bethesda, Maryland, designed and produced training materials and programs for Job Corps' National Health Program, and served as National Coordinator of Public Education for the National High Blood Pressure Education Program.

Donna lives in Portland, Oregon, with her husband, Dale Haller. She continues to work on a number of health-related projects as well as developing promotional materials for clients both within and outside the health care field. Artist/writer turned desktop publisher, Donna and I worked together to develop our unique approach to healthy and delicious Chinese menus. She served as editor for *A WOK A WEEK,* designed the layout, and set up the book on her desktop computer system.

draft # 412

NOW! ASAP! PRONTO

Bob Wilson, our Nutrient Analyst, is a remarkable fellow in many ways.

He is a person of meticulous precision. No discrepancy escapes his eye. He has ferreted out the nutrient content of ingredients not readily available in the computerized program, "Nutritionist[3]," (developed with a Western food bias,) and analyzed and reanalyzed each recipe.

Bob brings a light-hearted and kind spirit to all his work and interactions. This marvelous quality made the it much easier for Liz and Donna to grapple with the "fussy details" of the exacting science of nutrient analysis.

From his own life's experience, Bob has learned quite a bit about low-fat eating. Without dieting, he managed to change his lifestyle and lose 170 pounds. And he has maintained that loss for 25 years!

Bob holds a bachelors degree from Portland State University and is a Registered Dietetic Technician. He developed and heads up the nutritional analysis service for Kaiser Permanente and teaches in their weight management and cholesterol education programs. As a certified dietary interviewer, he assists in studies conducted by Kaiser's Health Research Center. His private weight management counseling business, *Light-Hearted Love, Whole Person Health*, continues to grow.

Bob, an avid gardener and a gourmet cook, lives and works in Portland, Oregon.

Nutritional Analysis Table

RECIPES	PER SERVING		
	CALORIES	CALORIES FROM FAT	% CALORIES FROM FAT
Asparagus Spears	46	13	26
Asparagus with Lotus Root	48	13	24
Baked Gourmet Beef Patties	127	34	28
Baked Prawns	79	7	9
Baked Turkey Cutlets	139	15	11
Banana Flambé	94	3	3
Bean Sprouts Fit for a King	58	14	23
Beef & Onions in Oyster Sauce	156	59	38
Beef on a Mongolian Grill	89	23	25
Braised Lamb with Leeks	210	53	26
Brown Rice	116	5	5
Chicken Fingers	100	24	24
Chicken on Skewers	52	8	15
Chicken with Anise & Peppercorns	176	47	28
Chinese Broccoli & Straw Mushrooms	80	13	16
Chinese Tossed Salad	24	2	7
Chinese Turkey Patties	128	21	17
Cold-tossed Noodles with Peanut Sauce	116	27	22
Crunchy Peapods	70	16	23
Cucumber Soup	57	11	20
Curried Shrimp on Bean Sprouts	164	46	28
Egg Drop & Spinach Soup	47	9	18
Eggplant in Savory Sauce	72	18	25
Fragrant Rice	99	8	9
Fruit on a Stick	54	3	4
Green Bean & Water Chestnut Salad	83	16	19

R E C I P E S	PER SERVING		
	CALORIES	CALORIES FROM FAT	% CALORIES FROM FAT
Hoisin Dipping Sauce	19	8	40
Honey Mustard Dipping Sauce	25	2	6
Hot & Spicy Dipping Sauce	5	0	4
Ivory & Jade Flowers	74	20	25
Lettuce Wraps with Beef & Glassy Noodles	167	34	20
Lettuce Wraps with Chicken & Mushrooms	105	28	26
Meatballs in Hot & Spicy Sauce	167	43	26
Noodles in Broth	102	10	9
Noodles with Bean Sprouts & Scallions	143	28	20
Noodles with Onion & Tomato Sauce	131	24	18
Peapod, Egg, Tomato & Mushroom Salad	99	18	18
Poached Fish Fillets with Ginger & Scallions	138	38	29
Poached Pears with Raspberry Sauce	61	3	5
Pork Chops Baked in Hoisin Sauce	195	58	30
Quick Honey & Peanut Dipping Sauce	64	37	54
Quick Sweet & Sour Dipping Sauce	40	0	0
Rice with a Tropical Flair	164	25	15
Rice with Crabmeat & Mushrooms	204	26	13
Rice with Spinach & Carrots	104	8	7
Roasted Pork Chops	175	60	35
Salmon Fillets with Hunan Chili Paste	212	74	35
Scallops & Shrimp with Hoisin Sauce	153	41	28
Seafood Firepot	140	9	7
Sesame Noodles	112	29	26
Sesame Sirloin Meatballs	117	43	38
Shanghai String Bean Salad	64	17	25
Shrimp Bisque	137	26	19
Shrimp on a Mongolian Grill	41	3	8

RECIPES	PER SERVING		
	CALORIES	CALORIES FROM FAT	% CALORIES FROM FAT
Shrimp on a Stick	76	6	9
Sichuan Chicken (dark meat)	139	31	23
(white meat)	159	14	9
Sichuan Noodles	91	13	14
Sichuan Beef on Skewers	26	6	23
Spicy Steamed Shrimp	98	7	7
Spinach & Mushrooms with Garlic	57	16	28
Steamed Shao Mais	191	22	11
Steamed Turkey Meatballs	176	26	15
Stir-tossed Cabbage with Ginger	72	20	27
Stir-tossed Potato & Carrot Sticks	194	35	17
Sweet & Sour Fish	219	60	28
Sweet & Sour Shrimp	218	55	25
Sweet Sugar Snap Peas	66	18	27
A Taste of Spring	52	6	10
Tofu with Crab & Straw Mushrooms	105	26	25
Tofu Salad with Peapods & Pepper	65	20	30
Tofu Salad with Sesame Seeds, Peas & Capers	113	27	24
Tofu Salad with Shrimp	98	31	31
Tomato & Glassy Noodle Soup	70	8	11
Turkey Wontons with Water Chestnuts & Cilantro	151	25	16
Turkey Vegetable Soup (with meat)	96	23	23
(without meat)	27	1	3
Vegetable Wontons	145	14	10
Vegetarian Firepot	124	21	16
White Rice	113	0	0

Index